Indian Peak Descents

Ski Mountaineering and Snowboarding In Colorado's Indian Peaks

Ron Haddad & Eileen Faughey

Foreword by Brian Litz

Disclaimer

Backcountry skiing and ski and snowboard mountaineering are hazardous. People have been injured or killed pursuing these activities. This book is not intended to teach you the skills that are needed to reduce the risk of accidental injury or death. It is solely intended to point the way to a variety of ski mountaineering routes. Only regular visits to the mountains can help you acquire the various skills that are needed to succeed in meeting your objectives.

We have made every effort to verify the data and the route descriptions. Despite our best efforts, errors may exist. If you discover any errors, we would appreciate learning about them. The authors assume no responsibility for problems that may arise from using this book.

Photography, map drawings and book design by the authors except where credited.

Printed in the United States

ISBN: 0-9650412-0-4

Published by Sigma Books, P.O. Box 21175 Boulder, Colorado 80308

Front Cover: Ron Haddad skiing "The Snake," Elk Tooth (12,848').
Title Page: Eileen Faughey ascends "Devil's Thumb Mountain" (12,650').
          "Caribou Peak" (12,923') is in the background.
Back Cover: Indian Peaks Wilderness west of Hessie.

Dedication

This guidebook is dedicated to Frederick M. Golomb, whose lifelong love for skiing and for high places continues to inspire in us and in others the essential attitude of the ski mountaineer.

Fred ascending Flagstaff Mountain in Utah's Wasatch Mountains

CONTENTS

The Indian Peaks In June
Central Part Of The Range

(View west from the high plains of Boulder County)

Peter Bridge

Mount Eva

Foreword

Chris Bonington, the great British mountaineer and explorer once wrote that no matter what adventures and sports you participate in during your lifetime, you will always return to the formative activities of your youth. If your sporting life began with rock climbing on small crags, then deep down you will always be a rock climber. If you spent your earliest mountain days tramping through the woods on skis, you will always be a skier at heart.

I believe the same relationship exists between people and the wilderness landscapes where the explorer or mountaineer in them began to blossom. No matter how small or great those mountains were, you will always be spiritually intertwined with wherever it was you gained your first summit, or savored your first one-pot meal, or hooted and hollered after that first perfect powder run, or broke your first binding, or watched a Camp Robber steal your lunch, or saw your first alpenglow.

For me that place is the Indian Peaks, that north-south jagged line of summits to the north and west of Denver and Boulder. Although humble in comparison with the great ranges of the world, the Indian Peaks are a complete alpine wilderness packed year-round with enough adventures and challenges to wear out an awful lot of gear. Lord knows I've trashed some equipment over the years, in every season, on these windy, rocky islands.

Recently, more and more people, mostly snow lovers who can't come to grips with the arrival of summer, have rediscovered the Indian Peaks – on skis. In fact, the peaks are gaining quite a reputation for having some of the finest spring ski mountaineering. They are also becoming a favorite haunt for Front Range snowboarders. The list of Indian Peak spring superlatives is long: they're close to major Front Range cities; the approaches are relatively short; there is a variety of terrain for skiers of all abilities; and, best of all, when compared with skiing here in the winter months, there is *less wind!* Hooray!

No one knows any better than Ron Haddad and Eileen Faughey, a friendly Front Range couple who have devoted a healthy portion of their spring and summer weekends over the past six years to exploring all of the hidden treasures tucked into the alpine basins and slopes of these inviting peaks. So whether you are an old hand or an Indian Peaks greenhorn, I invite you to grab your skis or snowboard, some sunscreen, and this revealing new guidebook, and enjoy a Colorado – make that American – treasure.

Brian Litz, Editor *BackCountry* magazine

Preface

In June of 1983 I organized a summer skiing "expedition" to Colorado with a few students and staff from the eastern boarding school where I was teaching. I had heard that snow lingered around Loveland Pass and other high spots well into June. A patrolman at Arapahoe Basin had described to me a unique snowy substance that forms in the spring. He called it "velvet corn." This was not to be confused, he went on, with the pebbly corn snow that is a springtime aberration at ski resorts. I was further inspired by a photo of the couloir on Castle Peak's north face that I had seen in a guidebook. In contrast with the west, spring and summer skiing is a rarity in the east, confined to a handful of locales in upstate New York, New Hampshire and Maine. We simply had to head west to extend the ski season – and we did.

Loaded with hundreds of tons of downhill skiing gear, camping supplies and movie filming equipment, and hyperventilating madly, we postholed from the Loveland Pass parking area at 11,990 feet westward along the Continental Divide. It was around 10:00 am. Our skis were lashed to our flimsy framepacks with avalanche cord, and they required frequent retieing. After an hour of trudging, we arrived at a gorgeous and reasonably consolidated south facing, steep snow slope. It was crowned with a modest, but still impressive, cornice which provided a convenient launch ramp. The four teenagers promptly donned boots and skis, launched off the cornice, and landed on the slope below with varying degrees of gracefulness. The two adults cautiously sidestepped onto the slope below. Several hundred feet below we found a flat, snow–free bench and set up camp directly below the steep snow slope we had just skied.

That afternoon we ventured away from camp and sank to our hips in snow that had been consolidated earlier. We employed a novel quadrupedal mode of snow travel in order to return to our camp. That night and all of the next day it snowed a foot. We heard and later saw several fresh snowslides. On the third day we reclimbed the slope above our camp and frolicked and filmed some more. Finally, we skied out to the highway, a short distance from the Arapahoe Basin Ski Area.

A less knowledgeable and more gleeful group of skiers would have been hard to come by in the summer of 1983. We exemplified the adage, "Ignorance is bliss." Since that carefree time and scores of trips later, we've come to appreciate the seriousness of mountain travel, the need for intelligent planning, and an awareness of hazards. The only thing that hasn't changed is the intensity of our love for mountain skiing. It is our hope that this book engenders and sustains in you a similar appreciation and passion.

Ron Haddad, 1996

Two flatlanders wallow in three feet of unconsolidated slush and think it's fun.

Introduction

The Indian Peaks

Driving west toward Boulder, one cannot resist gazing up at the snow-covered Indian Peaks rising high above the foothills. Shadowed on the north by towering Longs Peak in Rocky Mountain National Park, the Indian Peaks stretch southward for 27 miles and constitute the crest of the Continental Divide in this part of Colorado. Located about an hour, more or less, from Denver or Boulder, they are among the most accessible high mountains found near an urban population center. The forty summits that stretch from the National Park boundary on the north to Berthoud Pass on the south range in elevation from 12,000 to 13,500 feet. From October through July, the avid skier or snowboarder looks up at the Indian Peaks and dreams of the possibilities for descents among these snowy heights.

The Indian Peaks are snowcovered during most of the year. Even in late summer, isolated pockets of snow can be found. In absolute terms, the amount of snow that falls directly onto the Indian Peaks and, more broadly, the Front Range is unimpressive when compared with some other western ranges such as the San Juans, Wasatch, Sierras or Cascades. However, winter snow is transported eastward by prevailing winds which are accelerated by the gradually upsloping terrain west of the Divide. These ferocious winter winds scour snow from windward slopes and deposit and compact the snow on leeward slopes east of the Divide. These are the snows that one sees plastered onto the steep mountain faces and glacial cirques that are the hallmark of east slope topography above timberline.

Until about the middle of April, the snow above timberline consists of crusty sheets of impregnable *sastrugi*, the result of ruthless battering by the wind. As spring progresses the days lengthen, the sun rises higher and temperatures increase. Surface snow begins to melt and water percolates deeper into the snowpack and changes the structure of snow crystals from more crystalline, cohesive forms to more rounded, less cohesive forms. At night temperatures drop below freezing and the snowpack freezes solid again as ice grains become welded to their neighbors only to be remelted the following day. Freeze, melt…freeze, melt. Throughout May and into June and July, this cycle gradually transforms the snowpack into a consolidated and uniform mass with very little free air between the ice grains. It is the upper few inches of this consolidated snowpack that softens by day and forms corn snow. To skiers and snowboarders, "velvet corn" is the springtime equivalent of winter's "champagne powder." Slopes that had been either too avalanche prone or too windpacked to ski in winter are safer now and skiable.

But to view the Indian Peaks only as a place to ski or to snowboard is to miss the point of ski mountaineering. Like mountaineering in general, ski mountaineering is a multifaceted experience. There is joy to be found in the approach, in kicking steps up a snow slope, in summit views, in camaraderie, in spotting wildlife and wildflowers, as well as in the descent itself. Days are long and the sun warms the breezes. Subalpine forests are redolent with the vapor of minty resins. Streams are thunderous and swollen with meltwater. Savor the complete mountain environment and your ski descents will acquire a broader context and a more lasting meaning.

The purpose of this book is to enable skiers and snowboarders who possess at least intermediate skills to locate ski descent routes, to plan approaches sensibly, and to develop a heightened appreciation of these mountains. Advanced and expert skiers and snowboarders will find many challenging routes described in this guide. This book is not a "how to" guide. There are books and videos listed in the Appendix that can help you with technique, outdoor skills, and equipment.

One of us (R.H.) has skied every route in this book. Therefore, the temptation to designate particular routes as "classic" or "recommended" is great. The decision not to recommend certain routes stems from our desire to let readers develop an "eye" for the better routes and to form their own opinions. As you become more familiar with the Indian Peaks, you will spot routes that haven't been described in this book, and you may return to ski these secret spots.

The Indian Peaks Wilderness Area

The centerpiece of the Indian Peaks is the 73,391 acre Indian Peaks Wilderness Area (IPWA) which is contiguous with Rocky Mountain National Park to the north. The IPWA includes portions of Arapaho National Forest and Roosevelt National Forest. The IPWA includes, in addition to the peaks themselves, an abundance of forests, rushing streams, fifty lakes, stretches of alpine tundra, and wildlife. To the outdoor enthusiast this Wilderness is a cherished resource of inestimable value.

In 1978 Congress designated the Indian Peaks as a Wilderness Area. As with all Wilderness areas the intent was to protect the pristine condition and ecological values inherent in this part of Colorado. To this end, human intrusion and amenities have been minimized or eliminated. To the north, however, Rocky Mountain National Park is sustained by a different value structure. While the Park places a high value on resource preservation, it is also committed to the concept of accessibility to the public. Roads, interpretive displays, visitors' centers, campgrounds and other amenities exist to enable the public to get close to the wilderness. The distinction between a Wilderness Area and a National Park is an important one. Wilderness Areas such as the Indian Peaks are set aside to serve the wilderness. National Parks are designed to serve people.

Spring meltwater

The Wilderness Act of 1964 describes a Wilderness area as a place where:

> *"...the earth and its community of life are untrammeled by man, where man himself is a visitor who does not remain...and which (1) generally appears to have been affected primarily by the forces of nature, with the imprint of man's work substantially unnoticeable; (2) has outstanding opportunities for solitude or a primitive and unconfined type of recreation;"*

As we hike, camp, climb, ski or snowboard in the IPWA, we need to accept the fact that we are visitors. It is essential that we minimize our impacts. The IPWA's proximity to four urban centers (Denver, Boulder, Greeley, and Fort Collins) has made the Indian Peaks one of the most heavily traveled Wilderness areas in the nation. Current and future levels of use will only be acceptable if each visitor is knowledgeable about minimum-impact travel and camping techniques and about the regulations that permit or prohibit camping and campfires. There are portions of the Indian Peaks, such as the Four Lakes Travel Zone west of

Brainard Lake, where camping has been prohibited or is extremely restricted. These restrictions are necessary in order to preserve the qualities that draw us to these mountains in the first place.

Mark of the wilderness. A bear paw print along the Buchanan Pass Trail

Wilderness Regulations

Between June 1 and September 15 a permit is required to camp in the IPWA. Permits are issued at several locations that are listed in the Appendix. During 1995 the cost of a permit was five dollars per party. Permits may be obtained in advance by contacting one of the permit issuing locations. Along with your permit you will receive information about regulations.

The City of Boulder Watershed

If you look at a map of the Indian Peaks Wilderness Area, you will notice that a "bite" has been taken out of the east side of the Wilderness Area. This is the 6500 acre City of Boulder Watershed. This land is owned by the City of Boulder. The area is bounded on the north by Niwot Ridge and Navajo Peak and on the west and south by the Arapaho Peaks and the immense east shoulder of South Arapaho. The Watershed includes the relatively large Arapaho Glacier which is a prominent landmark when viewed from Boulder and points further east. Entry into the Watershed is prohibited by law. The area is patrolled regularly and trespassers will be fined.

Many skiers and snowboarders have spotted the Arapaho Glacier from the Arapaho Peaks or from afar and have been tempted by thoughts of a descent. The Front Range is sufficiently vast, and there are skiing opportunities to last a lifetime. Forgoing the pleasure of one more ski run is a small price to pay for preserving a unique and pristine watershed.

Clockwise: Blue Columbine, Fairyslipper, and Globe-flower. Just three of the many beautiful wildlflowers that bloom in the Indian Peaks

Equipment

The purpose of this section is to discuss only the equipment that is relevant to ski and snowboard mountaineering. It is not intended to contain an exhaustive list of items that one needs to pack for a trip. As with any backcountry endeavor, equipment choices are extremely important in ski mountaineering. While there are no hard and fast rules regarding equipment choices, one thing is certain. Equipment that is inadequate or that fails can, at the very least, cause delays during a trip. At worst, it can result in serious injury.

Nordic Skiing Equipment

For skiers who are looking for a combination of comfort, lightness, efficiency, and performance, the best choice is nordic equipment, also known as "free-heel" or "telemark" gear. Of course, an obvious requisite is that you know how to execute telemark turns, parallel turns and other useful maneuvers with free heels. However, you should not be

Free-heel boots, cable bindings, and skis

discouraged from fulfilling your ski mountaineering dreams just because you are not an "expert" free-heel skier. Many of the routes in this book can be enjoyed by budding free-heelers. Other routes require advanced techniques such as step-tellies and jump turns. It is worth noting in view of some of the opinions expressed below that all of the descent routes in this book can and have been skied with lightweight free-heel skis, cable bindings, and leather lace-up boots that are well suited for both uphill and downhill skiing.

During the past few years there has been an increase in sales of heavy free-heel skis and boots. Once the equipment of choice for telemark racing, this heavier nordic gear has found its way to the ski resorts and even the backcountry. In our opinion it is not necessary in the backcountry to use wider and heavier free-heel boards and stiff, heavy plastic or plastic plus leather boots. This equipment is a burden to carry or to ski on during the approach. If you are intent on advancing and refining your backcountry skiing skills, spend the time and effort required to learn to ski well using lighter equipment. Lighter weight equipment enhances your "feel" of the snow, is more maneuverable, allows for quicker more dance-like movements, is noticeably lighter when carried on a pack, and is a pleasure to use when skiing uphill. All of this translates into greater efficiency over the course of an entire day – a concept that seems to have been lost in the hype over more alpine-like nordic gear. Free-heel skis (without bindings) range in weight from 5.5 to 7.5 pounds.

The current variety of free-heel skis is bewildering compared with skis from ten years ago. Like downhill skis, each model varies in weight, internal construction, torsional rigidity, flex, sidecut, and surface area (flotation). It is unlikely that you will be purchasing skis strictly for spring ski descents, so select a ski that works well in the conditions that you expect to encounter during the entire winter and spring. That means every condition! The truth is that any free-heel ski with an alpine flex (single camber) and sidecut will work in corn snow. Ski construction matters more on very steep snow that hasn't softened. For such snow it is helpful to have a torsionally stiffer and a wider ski. The extra width helps to keep the "wings" of your bindings from catching in the snow. We can see that this discussion is leading nowhere, so maybe we should move on to something else like bindings and boots.

Choosing a binding is a bit simpler. The choices are 75 mm three-pin bindings which have prevailed for eons; three-pin bindings with cables that wrap around the heel of the boot; and cable-bindings without three-pins. Releasing systems are available for all of these types. Ski leashes are absolutely essential since it is possible, even with combination pin/cable bindings, to become disconnected from a ski. Bindings range in weight from less than a pound to 1.5 pounds.

Three-pin bindings are the lightest and least expensive choice. However, three-pin bindings can malfunction for three reasons: the pin holes in the boot can become lodged with dirt, pebbles, or ice during a hike in; pin holes can rip out, or the boot sole can fracture near the pin holes; or, least likely, the bail that clamps down on the boot can break or become unfastened.

Cable bindings are a bit heavier than three-pin bindings. However, the added weight hardly affects "swing weight" which is the perceived weight of the ski when a skier is turning the ski. Cable bindings hold the boot to the ski more securely. The popular notion that a normally-adjusted cable binding increases appreciably the torsional rigidity of the ski boot is not true. Torsional rigidity, which is an important property of any ski boot, is related to boot materials and construction.

With cable bindings the cable tension can be adjusted easily to provide a larger degree of up-down heel movement for approaches and for kicking and gliding or a smaller degree of heel movement for downhill skiing. Cables can break, and it is advisable to carry a spare on all outings. The combination three-pin and cable binding is especially bombproof and secure. One popular system has a readily detachable cable for increased freedom and decreased weight during approaches and ascents.

A completely different boot to ski attachment called "NNN-BC" has been slowly gaining ground during the past several years. This system utilizes a boot with a different toe that is compatible with only a NNN-BC binding. Initial assessments of this binding suggest that for ski mountaineering it offers no advantage over the more traditional bindings described above. NNN-BC bindings can be equipped with a releasing system.

Selecting boots for free-heel skiing is no longer easy. The unassuming, leather laceup boots that once were the mainstay of backcountry skiers are being crowded out by plastic, high-topped, forward-leaning, stiff-cuffed, buckled creations. Some of these boots weigh more than the lightest alpine-touring boots. (See below) Fortunately, the lighter, more comfortable leather laceup types are still available – but who knows for how long? As with lighter skis, we believe that lighter boots are an advantage during approaches and climbs, activities which make up 95% of the time spent on an outing.

Alpine Skiing Equipment

If you decide to use traditional, heavy alpine skis and boots, you will need to pack in your equipment until you reach the top of the descent route. Problems arise, however, when a descent route is preceded by a snowcovered trail or a lingering snowpack along a valley bottom. Since it is next to impossible to ski these sections without a free heel, postholing is the inevitable and grueling alternative, unless you use the equipment described below.

Alpine-Touring boots, bindings, and skis

A better choice for alpine skiers is to purchase alpine-touring (A.T.) skis, boots, and bindings. A.T. equipment is sold at some mountain shops and through several mail-order companies. A.T. skis are lighter and may be wider and shorter than those used at ski areas. They perform well under a variety of backcountry conditions (moguls are not among these). As with all ski equipment sold today, big savings in weight have been made by many manufacturers. Weight per pair of skis (without bindings) ranges from 6 to 9 pounds.

Traditional A.T. bindings consist of a plate or steel rails which the ski boot snaps into, much like a traditional binding. However, the plate is hinged at the front where it connects with the ski. The rear of the plate can be locked into the ski for skiing downhill. To ski the flats or uphill, one simply releases the back end of the plate which frees the heel to move up and down. A.T. bindings are capable of releasing during a fall although some models will do so more reliably than others.

A recent innovation in A.T. bindings dispenses altogether with the heavier rail/plate concept. Instead the binding toepiece consists of a hinge that clamps directly into the sides of the boot toe. The boot, which needs to be compatible with this toepiece, is now free to move up and down without being attached to a plate or rails. The result is a lighter system and a more ergonomic pivot point closer to one's toes. As with all A.T. bindings the boot heel can be locked down when skiing downhill. The weight per pair is 1.3 pounds. Conventional A.T. bindings weigh in between 3.5 and 5 pounds.

Regular downhill ski boots are not recommended for use with A.T. bindings. To go the complete A.T. route, you should purchase A.T. boots. These plastic boots are designed to snap into A.T. bindings. The sole is lugged and has a built in rocker for much easier climbing and walking without skis. These boots are light, 6 to 8 pounds as compared with 8 to 10 pounds for regular downhill boots, and since they are softer, are more comfortable. The cuff of an A.T. boot is releasable and generously hinged at the ankle allowing freedom of lower leg movement when one is shuffling along on an approach. Later the cuff can be locked into a forward leaning position for skiing down. Don't expect the above boot-binding-ski combination to provide the level of control you may be used to with regular downhill equipment. On the other hand, the convenience, comfort, and weight savings overshadow their performance liabilities.

Snowboards

The evolution in snow boards and technique over the past ten years has changed a herky jerky skidding motion into a fluid, carving style of descent that is both powerful and graceful. We have seen the number of riders toting boards into the backcountry increase steadily.

The obvious limitation for snowboarders is their inability to shift their boards into uphill mode. This problem can be solved by using snowshoes which, along with every other piece of outdoor equipment, have been cast in ultralight designs. Using a pack that is designed to carry a snowboard and approaching on small, lightweight snowshoes, snowboarders can access the same backcountry routes as skiers.

Snowboarders who plan on skiing steeper routes should carry an ice axe to use when ascending or descending. When ascending, the ice axe is helpful for balance and anchoring between steps and for performing a self arrest if a slip occurs. During descents the ice axe should be held in one hand by its head so that it is available for a self arrest.

Why does the issue of weight figure so heavily in this discussion of equipment? First, ski mountaineering and backcountry skiing are physically demanding activities. Second, as the snow recedes into the alpine basins and couloirs in late spring and summer, you are forced to pack in your ski gear. Except for the demigods whose extraordinary skiing feats are heralded in ski publications, the rest of us mortals have limited muscle glycogen and energy reserves. Ascending a steep snowfield with overweight equipment strapped to a bulky pack may look good in pictures and may even be necessary in some situations, but it is exhausting. Opt for the lightest setup that allows you to ski a slope safely and enjoyably, and steer clear of the advertising hype. As with all backcountry modes of travel, it makes sense to travel as efficiently as possible to maximize your success rate and enjoyment–without compromising on safety and dependability of equipment.

Miscellaneous Equipment

Skins – Ski skins enable you to travel uphill – steeply uphill. They are like having four wheel drive plus chains on your feet. (A well kept secret is that some of us even engage our skins when descending scary wooded trails with unmentionable snow conditions.) Ski skins attach using either straps or a layer of glue. Glue-ons currently are outselling strap-ons. Unquestionably glue-ons are harder to maintain and to recondition, and they require a great deal of t.l.c. However, a well maintained pair will provide years of dependable use. Skins come with either plastic, nylon, or mohair gripping surfaces. Nylon and mohair provide much better glide than do plastic skins. There is not enough overall difference between nylon versus mohair to proclaim a winner in this category. Skins are available for alpine and for nordic widths of skis. Consider a tail attachment retrofit if one is not provided with the skins you are purchasing. With glue-ons touching up the glue is necessary once or twice a year with total regluing needed less frequently. Regluing can be a nightmare unless you know the secret method. Ask an experienced salesperson at your favorite mountain shop for the latest regluing method. Don't forget to pick up a tube of glue when you purchase your skins.

Climbing skins

Ski poles with self-arrest grips

Poles – Adjustable ski poles are among the great innovations in skiing. They can be extended to increase arm thrust when kicking and gliding, shortened to normal length for skiing downhill, and greatly shortened when kicking steps up a steep slope. You can purchase poles with self-arrest grips. You can also purchase these grips separately to attach to your poles. Self-arrest grips are like mini-ice axes for each hand. They are helpful climbing aids when the going gets very steep, but they are not a substitute for an ice axe should a fall occur on a very steep slope. It is a good idea to practice using them in a variety of controlled situations to get a feel for what their capabilities are.

Heel Lifts – These have been standard equipment on A.T. bindings for years. Recently we began using heel lifts on our nordic skis for skinning up steep stretches of snow. We found them to be fantastic! By reducing the degree of flexion between our feet and lower legs, skinning uphill has become more pleasant, much less of a chore, and more efficient. We recommend them highly. The additional weight is negligible.

Packs – Few who spend a lot of time in the backcountry would disagree that a well designed pack is like a reliable companion. A pack should be compatible with your needs and traveling habits. There are several excellent packs available for backcountry skiing. Look for a pack with a shovel compartment, straps along the sides for attaching skis, a generously padded hipbelt for comfort and for stability when skiing downhill, and sufficient capacity for emergency supplies and extra clothing, food, and water.

Gaiters – Consider keeping a pair of full boot gaiters ("supergaiters") attached to leather boots all year. A bead of Shoe Goo along the welt of the boot prevents the rubber rand of the gaiter from sliding off the toe. Gaiters keep boots free of snow, add a bit of warmth, and protect boots from nicks. These nicks can occur when executing a less than perfect turn in which the sharp edge of one ski rides onto the opposite boot.

Kneepads – Free-heel skiers should wear knee pads during descents. In the spring a slope that appears uniformly covered by deep snow can be deceptive. Many of the routes are in scree and talus filled gullies. It is possible for a ski to slice down onto a hidden block of talus and cause a shattering blow to the knee.

Altimeter – For orienteering in unfamiliar terrain and for monitoring progress during an ascent, an altimeter is useful in conjunction with a topographic map and a compass. A digital wristwatch/altimeter is available that reads at ten foot intervals and has other useful "bells and whistles."

Clothing – Carry two pairs of gloves – a very light pair of liners and a heavier pair of ski gloves. The liners are useful early in the morning when the air is chilly. The ski gloves are necessary when skiing downhill in order to protect hands from abrasions in the event of a fall. Despite its wonderful qualities, corn snow is insidiously abrasive against unprotected skin.

A cap with a bill keeps the sun out of your eyes. A heavier winter ski cap or a balaclava keeps the cold out of your head. It can get very cold very fast at any time of the year. A baseball cap is meager protection against hail or sleet.

A cotton shirt and shorts may be suitable for a hot summer approach. But if you do not have a dry set of clothing to replace your sweat-soaked items, you are setting yourself up for hypothermia if the weather changes for the worse. Late morning or afternoon thunderstorms accompanied by wind, sleet and plunging temperatures are common in the Rockies.

It isn't necessary to wear the latest brightly-colored garments with "Extreme" written on each to be comfortable. Your best bet is to carry several thin layers made of synthetic fabric or wool with a breathable waterproof parka and pants as the outer layer. This is old but sound advice that provides maximum comfort and versatility.

The Ten Essentials:

- map of area in zip-loc bag
- compass
- flashlight with spare batteries and bulb
- extra food and water
- extra clothing
- sunglasses
- first aid kit
- pocket knife
- matches in waterproof container
- fire starter

Mountain Hazards

Snowslides – Earlier in our introduction we described the freeze-melt cycle that transforms steep avalanche-prone slopes into more stable, consolidated snow that is safer to climb and to ski. In spite of the greater stability of the spring snowpack, the mountaineer needs to be aware that dangers still exist especially during April and May. During these transitional months large amounts of water may accumulate between the ground and the snow. Given a suitable bed surface and slope angle on which to slide, dangerous wet slabs with the consistency of cement can result. Once in late spring we observed the aftermath of a huge slab avalanche that ran along the ground just above treeline on an incline of 25 degrees. Along similar lines, smooth rock slabs that lie tilted above one's route can readily unload their snowcover as the rock warms and becomes lubricated with meltwater. Careful route selection and timing are essential to avoid this hazard which increases as the day progresses.

Colorado's winters are notorious for posing a high slab avalanche hazard. With the onset of spring, the chances of slab avalanches occurring become less. But then it is not unusual for five to ten inches of fresh snow to fall on top of consolidated snow in late May and early June usually above 10,000 feet. For a day or two after such a storm the danger of slab avalanches reappears on slopes near or above 30 degrees. Even when complete consolidation of the snowpack finally occurs, mountaineers must still maintain their guard. We have observed both slow and fast sluffs of heavy wet corn snow in June, typically during sunny afternoons or during a pounding bout of hail. Sluffing may be triggered by a skier especially when the snow has had a chance to soften to a depth of four to six inches. Unlike slab avalanches, sluffs lack cohesion and are usually innocuous. However, their weight makes them capable of knocking a person off balance. The observant mountaineer stays abreast of the weather history in the area of interest and constantly studies the terrain for evidence of past avalanche activity and for signs of potential avalanche hazard. When approaching a slope that appears prone to sluffing, it is wise to proceed cautiously.

An enormous June wet slide probably triggered by a collapsed cornice. Notice that the bed surface is composed of smooth rock.

Cornices – The prevailing westerly winds that transport huge amounts of snow across the Divide are responsible for the buildup of cornices on ridgetops. Cornices can transform ridgetops into beautiful abstract sculptures. Cornices that break are another matter. Even small cornices are extremely heavy. Those that overhang precariously are very likely to break sometime during the spring. It is common to see crate-sized blocks of fractured cornices on many of the slopes described in this book. The number and size of these blocks is a sobering testament to the size of the original cornice. It is easy to envision the outcome of an encounter with a collapsing wall of snow. The careful mountaineer is constantly vigilant when climbing or skiing below cornices. It is best to avoid exposure altogether even if doing so involves selecting a more circuitous route. If it is necessary to climb beneath an overhanging cornice, try to predict the path that the falling snow might take down the slope – and try to stay out of this danger zone.

Cornices such as this one are a significant hazard to mountaineers.

Rockfall – Another hazard of spring mountain travel is rockfall. Anyone who has traveled in the mountains during the spring has probably heard the clattering of rock fall. During the winter water seeps into cracks in rocks and freezes. Expansion of the ice exerts tremendous lateral pressure on the surrounding rock causing it to fracture. As the ice that holds the rocks in place thaws, the loosened rocks are free to find a more stable resting place. Later in the summer many slopes will be littered with rock fragments that broke free earlier as a result of frost action on surrounding rock faces. Crude calculations suggest that rock fall in some zones is a daily occurrence during the spring. The presence of rocks under skis can make for an unpleasant descent. The presence of rocks careening overhead can be deadly!

Moats – Like their medieval counterparts, moats that separate rock walls from the snow are meant to be avoided. Caused by the differential melting of the snow adjacent to rock walls, moats are a common sight throughout the spring and summer seasons. No one deliberately skis into a moat, but it is easy to see how one bad turn might launch a skier moatward with serious consequences. Take note of their presence as you ascend a route.

Crater Lake Couloir (South Boulder Creek Region). This route is threatened by (1) a cornice, part of which has already broken, (2) a moat where the snow meets the warmer rock, and (3) rockfall.

Snow "Burn" – A surprising characteristic of corn snow is its abrasive quality. The granules of ice that comprise spring snow have the quality of coarse sandpaper. Even a slow speed slide with skin exposed can cause a painful abrasion which at first will not feel painful because of the anesthetic action of the cold snow. On one June outing in the Maroon Bells-Snowmass Wilderness, a companion of ours received an extensive abrasion along his midriff while glissading down a slope. The affected skin was precisely where his hip belt was designed to rest. While it may be sporting to ski in shorts and a tee shirt, one should not leave skin exposed when skiing a slope where there is a chance of falling.

Sunburn – Brilliant sunshine and long days are certainly among the joys of summer in the mountains. Unfortunately alpine bowls behave as giant reflector ovens with mountaineers the unwitting foci of their reflections. Back-country skiers accustomed to the cold temperatures and lower sun angles of winter frequently learn the hard way just how hot and sunny alpine bowls can get. Severe sunburn invariably results from a failure to apply – and reapply – sunscreen. Neither of us can forget the second degree facial burns and subsequent blistering and peeling that we received during a trip through the High Sierras in July at a time when we were inexperienced. All exposed skin surfaces should be slathered generously with sunscreen. Long-sleeved shirts and windpants provide greater protection from the sun. To reduce overhead glare a cap with a bill should be worn. Include sunglasses with side guards ("glacier glasses") and you should be adequately protected. Lip balm with sunscreen should be applied frequently throughout the day. Don't be fooled on overcast days. Ultraviolet rays can penetrate clouds and fog.

Lightning – Late morning and afternoon thunderstorms are common in the Indian Peaks during the summer. Storms develop and move in amazingly fast. Freezing rain, sleet, and hail accompanied by high winds and plummeting temperatures are the norm during these storms. By far the greatest hazard during a thunderstorm is lightning. Deaths from lightning strikes occur in the mountains every year. There is nothing more frightening than being trapped on or near a summit with lightning striking nearby. Every mountain traveler should know the procedures to follow during a lighting storm. Weather forecasts can be helpful in judging the likelihood of thunderstorms on a given day; but despite the rosiest forecast, storms may still develop locally. The best policy for avoiding storms is to start out early, summit and descend before noon, and spend the afternoon enjoying a leisurely return to the trailhead or to camp.

Peter Bridge

Lightning and dense fog force a return to the trailhead.

Dehydration – It is common knowledge that dehydration can be a serious problem when exercising at higher elevations. And yet most mountaineers become dehydrated to some degree in the course of a day. The main reasons for insufficient water intake are: the inconvenience of stopping to remove one's pack and drink; the extra poundage involved in carrying plenty of water; and the fact that the thirst sensation in humans is delayed until a person is already mildly dehydrated. Here are some strategies to avoid these problems. Start your water intake when you wake up and continue drinking up to a liter before you arrive at the trailhead. In addition to carrying one to two liters in your pack, carry a half-liter water bottle on your hipbelt within arms reach and take sips during the approach. Before beginning a steep final pitch, take a ten minute break to gobble some food and drink some more.

Before concluding this section it is worth reemphasizing the importance of starting out early as a way to help avoid some of the problems that were described above. By traveling during the early morning hours the snow will be firmer and less likely to slide or sluff. Rockfall and cornice breakage are less likely especially if temperatures have dropped below freezing the night before. Since it is cooler in the morning, physical exertion is more comfortable and less taxing. By summiting before noon, there is a better chance that the top layer of snow will have thawed just enough for perfect skiing conditions. Snow that consists of deep slush is a nuisance to ski. Leaving the trailhead at seven o'clock should be early enough for routes in the Indian Peaks that have relatively short approaches. Six o'clock is the recommended starting time for longer approaches. A few of the routes described can be enjoyed more fully by backpacking into a basecamp the day before and getting an early start the next day. By spending the night closer to one's destination, it is possible to ski two or three nearby routes during the morning and early afternoon.

Explanation of Route Summaries

Each route description begins with a summary that provides information needed for choosing and planning a trip. Here is an explanation of the subheadings that appear with each summary.

Route Title – The route title is usually the name of the mountain where the descent route is located. Occasionally the route title refers to a geographical feature that is not part of any particular mountain – for example, *Skyscraper Glacier* or *King Lake Bowls*.

If the name of a mountain is in quotation marks, this means that the name is unofficial and does not appear on the U.S.G.S. map. Some of these unofficial names are the ones that Gerry Roach used in his book, *Indian Peaks Wilderness Area,* while others were named by us. Similarly, a few of the names of descent routes were borrowed from Gerry's book while most other route names are ours.

Starting Elevation – This is the elevation at the parking area suggested in the Access Points section.

Elevation Gain – This is the *net* gain in elevation computed by subtracting the starting elevation from the elevation given in the route title. Occasionally a route may involve a small loss of elevation which is noted in the route description. However, these losses are not significant enough to be worth computing.

Distance – This is the round trip distance in miles from the suggested parking area to the high point on the route. Measurements were taken from the U.S.G.S. maps using a map measurer. Actual distances may vary slightly. No travel times have been suggested since it has been our experience that these vary enormously among different parties. One half to a full day should be allowed for most of the routes.

U.S.G.S. Map(s) – This is the title of the 7.5 minute U.S.G.S. map. Certain maps are more popular than others so it is wise to call distributors ahead of time to check on availability. See the Appendix for names of distributors.

Access Point – This is the closest town or settlement that serves as a landmark for locating the trailhead. For routes that lie east of the Continental Divide the access points are situated along or near the Peak-To-Peak Highway. Only one access point (Monarch Lake) is located west of the Continental Divide. Three of the access points lie a short distance north of Interstate 70 near Idaho Springs. Detailed information about access points and directions to trailheads from access points is provided in the next section titled *Access Points.*

Best Month(s) – The routes described in this book may be skied in spring and summer after the snowpack has consolidated. March is definitely too early. The beginning of April is also too early for most of the routes. In late April some of the routes will be skiable while others are not safe to ski until June. The months given with each route are meant to give only a general idea of the best time to plan a trip. Almost all of the routes are skiable for several weeks to more than a month.

Several factors determine when and for how long a route is skiable. The depth of the winter's snowpack; the number and severity of spring snowstorms in the high country; the springtime average daily temperatures; and the amount of rainfall and cloud cover. It is not necessary to delve into these issues in detail. Instead a couple of examples from the past few years should make it clear that predicting the onset of spring consolidation can be tricky. In the spring and summer of 1993 there was above average winter snowfall. The spring weather was normal. Consolidation came on schedule in late May and June. Good skiing was had through early August. In 1994, the winter snow was almost average. April and May were hot and dry. In June the snow had the texture of July snow, that is, shallow corn on top of a hard icy base. July's snow was hard and treacherous with August almost snow free. In 1995 record amounts of snow fell during April and May. June saw a deep snowpack with an April consistency. Consolidation was delayed until July with good skiing through August.

The only surefire way to determine the condition of the spring snowpack is to go out and stand on it, or else talk to a reliable source who has been in the mountains recently.

Map – This is the page in this book where the U.S.G.S. excerpted map can be found. The map shows the descent route and may include the entire route from the trailhead. The maps in this book are not intended to substitute for the actual map, which should be studied and annotated as needed.

Rating – There are three difficulty ratings: *Intermediate, Advanced, and Expert*. The rating is determined by the steepest slope angle that is encountered on the descent route when the snow is in ideal condition.

- Intermediate - up to 25 degrees
- Advanced - 25 to 35 degrees
- Expert - 35 to 50 degrees

However, a very short (one or two turns) steep section is not significant enough to warrant a higher rating for a route. The rating is not based on the length or difficulty of the approach and subsequent climb. An intermediate route can be skied by a person who has fresh skiing skills. A solid telemark or parallel turn is required for advanced routes. A bombproof jump turn or step-telemark is required on expert routes where missing the mark is likely to result in a long slide.

An inclinometer was used to measure slope angles for many of the routes in this book. We also used a trigonometric formula to derive slope angles directly from U.S.G.S. 7.5 minute topographic maps. A "slopemeter" in the Appendix provides data so you can do this yourself.

Advanced and expert routes should be avoided when conditions are marginal. An icy or a rough surface due to insufficient thawing or aging of the snow surface can quickly turn an intermediate slope into an advanced one. Spend the time taking pictures, spotting wildlife, or chatting with friends. The snow will stick around until another day. Remember that a ski mountaineering excursion offers a lot more than skiing.

Off-route on Elk Tooth. "This is another fine mess you've gotten us into, Ron!"

Who said summer skiing is hard work?

A marmot, the hungry monarch of Mount Audubon

Access Points
(North to South)

The scenic, high elevation Peak To Peak Highway is the primary auto route east of the Continental Divide for travelers heading into the Indian Peaks. The highway winds southward from Estes Park to U.S. Highway 6, and ends two miles from Interstate 70 and seven miles east of Idaho Springs. The numbering of the Peak-To-Peak Highway can be confusing. From Estes Park southward to a fork four miles south of Allenspark, the highway is designated "Route 7." From this fork to Nederland the highway is "Route 72." From Nederland to U.S. Highway 6 through Clear Creek Canyon, the highway is "Route119."

For travelers accessing the west side of the Indian Peaks, there are two options: Interstate 70 to Highway 40 over Berthoud Pass, then north past Winter Park to Granby. Or, if it is open, one can take Trail Ridge Road (Highway 34) from Estes Park to Grand Lake through Rocky Mountain National Park.

"Hey, Eileen. Did you see my stuff anywhere?"

The first name in each Access Point is the main town situated along the Peak-To-Peak Highway (east of the Divide) or along Highway 40 (west of the Divide). The second name in the Access Point is where you can park to begin a tour.

The exact place where one chooses to park often depends on how snowbound or muddy a particular road is at a certain time of the year. Do not attempt to negotiate a road that is snowcovered or muddy. Doing so causes severe erosion of the road bed. There is only a slight time advantage when forcing a vehicle along a rough road since you must drive very slowly. In the spring a marginal road will usually end up being totally impassable after a mile or so.

Allenspark/Ski Bowl Road

From the point on the Peak-To-Peak Highway where "Route 72" becomes "Route 7," drive 3.3 miles further north and turn left (west) at the sign, "Allenspark-Ferncliff," into the community of Allenspark. At 0.9 mile make a left onto Ski Road (2WD dirt). Drive for 0.6 mile to a "T," turn left (still called Ski Road) and drive one mile west to a signed fork, "Rock Creek" (left) and "St. Vrain Mountain Trail" (right). Turn left and downhill on a rougher road, cross a side creek, and park one quarter mile ahead by a campsite on the north side of Rock Creek. If the Rock Creek road is in poor shape, you can also park back at the signed fork.

Streams that normally are easy to cross are often swollen with meltwater in the spring.

Peaceful Valley/Camp Dick Campground

Locate the hairpin turn slightly west of Peaceful Valley, a tiny settlement between Ward and Allenspark. Here the Peak-To-Peak Highway crosses Middle St. Vrain Creek. Turn west onto the dirt road and drive a mile to the Camp Dick campground where there is parking at the far end of the campground. Persons with high clearance 4WD may attempt to continue on the rough and rocky road for four miles to the St. Vrain Glacier Trailhead. In May and early June the road is closed because of snowcover and washouts. On the north side of Middle St. Vrain Creek there is a foot trail that leads to the same trailhead as the road. Either way the access is gentle but long.

Ward/Beaver Reservoir

From Ward drive north 2.6 miles and turn left (west) on a dirt road (a small sign says "Camp Tahosa"). Take this dirt road 2.8 miles to the signed Coney Flats Road on the right. This rocky road begins on the north side of Beaver Reservoir, and there is space for parking on the shoulder. The road, which is usually closed to vehicles due to its poor condition, climbs gently to the west and is flooded in spots. It reaches Coney Flats and the Wilderness trailhead after 3.5 miles. Be aware that the road has three major forks along its length. If you are on foot, which is likely, keep right at each of these forks.

Ward/Brainard Lake

The settlement of Ward lies a "stone's throw" east of the Peak-To-Peak Highway. About 100 yards north of the more northerly turnoff to Ward on the Peak-To-Peak Highway, take a hard left onto the paved road to Brainard Lake. After 2.7 winding miles you'll reach the Red Rock Lake Trailhead and gate closure. The gate is closed through May and opens sometime in June. Park here when the gate is closed.

Many people bemoan the road closure which lasts into June. But the two mile walk (or bike ride) to Brainard Lake is easy and very scenic. Use the time to bond with fellow adventurers or, if it's early, to appreciate the solitude. By midday the road will be much more crowded.

Sometime in June, when the road is finally opened to cars, you can drive past Brainard Lake and the Pawnee Campground to one of two well-signed and spacious backcountry trailheads. The more southerly trailhead (10,500') accesses Long Lake, Lake Isabelle, and the Pawnee Pass Trail. The more northerly one (10,480') accesses Mitchell and Blue Lakes and the trails to Mount Audubon, Paiute Peak, and Mount Toll. Visitors to the Brainard Lake area are charged a reasonable day-use fee.

The view west from Brainard Lake. The peaks that are visible from left to right are Navajo, Apache, Shoshoni, "Pawshoni," and Pawnee (just barely).

Nederland/Caribou

From the traffic circle in the center of Nederland, turn west onto the Peak-To-Peak Highway (Route 72W), drive 0.4 miles and turn left onto the 2WD dirt road to Caribou. Take this road 5.0 miles to its end at an overlook and the start of Forest Road 505.

Nederland/Fourth of July Trailhead

From the traffic circle in the center of Nederland, drive south 0.6 mile on the Peak-To-Peak highway and turn right (west) at a sign for Eldora. Stay on this valley road which leads to the tiny settlement of Eldora after three miles. This "Eldora" is different than the nearby ski area with the same name. Another mile and the pavement ends. Continue on the 2WD dirt road for 0.8 mile to a "Y". Take the signed right fork and drive a four miles to the rustic Buckingham Campground and Fourth of July Trailhead, and park in the trailhead parking area. The Arapaho Pass Trail begins here and leads 3.5 miles west to Arapaho Pass.

Nederland/Hessie Trailhead

Follow the directions above for Nederland/Fourth of July Trailhead. When you reach the "Y" intersection along the dirt road that leads west from the town of Eldora, take the left fork. This road is an often-flooded, high clearance 4WD road. Take it 0.3 mile to the Hessie townsite and park. Less amphibious travelers usually choose to park back at the "Y" and hike along a herd path through the forest on the north side of the flooded road.

From the townsite the official "Hessie Trailhead" is a short walk further west where a solid bridge crosses the North Fork of Middle Boulder Creek. This is an important (and busy) trailhead that accesses three major drainages and four trails: the Jasper Lake/Devil's Thumb Trail, the Woodland Lake Trail, the King Lake Trail, and the Lost Lake Trail.

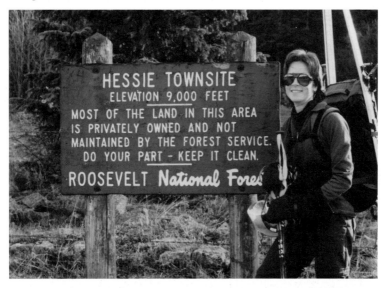

Rollinsville or Winter Park/Rollins Pass Road, Yankee Doodle Lake, and Forest Lakes Trailhead

From the traffic circle in Nederland head south on the Peak-To-Peak Highway (Route 119) for five miles to Rollinsville. Turn right (west) onto a 2WD dirt road. This road shares the broad valley of South Boulder Creek with the Denver & Rio Grand Railroad and with scattered log cabins and pastel-colored houses. The valley has an old-timey feel. At 7.6 miles the signed Rollins Pass Road turns right off the main road.

The Rollins Pass Road is a 2WD dirt road that used to make it possible to drive from Boulder County to Winter Park. The road crosses the open tundra of the Continental Divide at Rollins Pass (elevation 11,671'.) The road was once a railroad grade and so it contours extensively at a grade never exceeding 5%. It is only open during the summer after the snow has melted. The only glitch is in trying to drive to Rollins Pass from the east. The Needle's Eye Tunnel, situated above Yankee Doodle Lake and about 1.5 miles before the Pass, has been closed due to rock fall in the tunnel. In addition the two trestles that traverse the Devil's Slides, 0.5 mile before the pass, have been closed to vehicles as well. If you plan to approach Rollins Pass from the east, drive ten miles from the Rollins Pass Road turnoff and park by Yankee Doodle Lake. Then scramble up northwest to the road (this bypasses the tunnel) and walk the scenic remainder of the road to the Pass. The view north toward the wide alpine basin holding King, Bob and Betty Lakes as well as several steep descent routes is superb. The walk to the Pass provides a perfect opportunity to reconnoiter these routes.

The Forest Lakes Trailhead is 1.6 miles further from Yankee Doodle Lake, and the road to the trailhead may be blocked by snowdrifts at or beyond Yankee Doodle Lake. The Forest Lakes Trailhead is used for the Forest Lakes descent routes.

To reach Rollins Pass from Winter Park drive to Winter Park via U.S. 40 and Berthoud Pass and look for the sign for the Rollins Pass Road on the right side of the highway. It is 13.8 miles to the pass from Winter Park.

Rollinsville/East Portal

Follow the directions above to where the Rollins Pass Road turns right from the main road. Continue on the main dirt road 0.75 mile to the road's end and park 150 yards from the gaping maw of the Moffat Tunnel. This incredible edifice is the eastern portal of a tunnel that pierces the Continental Divide for a distance of six miles connecting Winter Park and the Fraser Valley with the eastern slope. If you're lucky, the tunnel will disgorge a train as you fiddle with your gear. To reach the South Boulder Creek trailhead (presently unsigned), walk toward the tunnel, turn left across the tracks, cross the creek and aqueduct on a bridge and turn west on the obvious wide trail into the woods.

Rollinsville/James Peak Lake Trailhead

This is an underutilized, high elevation trailhead that provides access to James Peak Lake and the spectacular east face of James Peak. A high clearance 4WD vehicle is needed to reach it. It is an alternative to the St. Mary's Glacier trailhead which bustles with people on weekends. Head west from Rollinsville (see above) on the 2WD dirt Rollins Pass Road for five miles to Tolland. Just past Tolland turn left onto FR 176 (4WD) which climbs into Mammoth Gulch and turns into FR 353. The road climbs steadily along the south rim of Mammoth Gulch across gently sloping meadows and some clearcuts. There are stupendous views of the east face of James Peak as well as the peaks above East Portal.

The condition of the road worsens the higher one goes. In June, at about mile 5 from Tolland (11,000') the road is likely to be blocked by intermittent snow drifts. If the road is passable at this point, bounce along toward the signed James Peak Lake Trailhead at 6.5 miles and park. If the road isn't passable, find a pullout, park, and walk the easy mile or two to the trailhead. Considering the poor condition of the road above 11,000', you won't waste much time by hiking instead of driving, and besides, the scenery is terrific. At the trailhead take a few minutes to study the east face of James Peak and the geography of Upper Mammoth Gulch. It takes about 45 minutes to drive from Tolland to the trailhead, so an especially early start is needed to account for this portion of the trip.

Fall River Road/Fall River Reservoir Road

Take I-70 west toward Idaho Springs. One mile past the last Idaho Springs exit, leave the interstate at Exit 238 "Fall River Road." Turn right (north) onto Fall River Road. After 6.4 miles there is a hairpin where the paved main road turns right. The dirt Fall River Reservoir Road (unmarked) continues straight ahead. Drive as far as possible on this road. Where you park will be determined by the time of the year and by the extent of the spring snowpack. In June it is usually possible to drive close to Fall River Reservoir.

Weekend warrior riding into battle

Fall River Road/Alice

The subdivision known as "Alice" is located 8.0 miles from the start of Fall River Road (see above). At mile 8.0 on the Fall River Road, locate the dirt RD 275. Turn left and continue 0.9 mile to Stewart Road which forks right. Continue as far as possible on Stewart Road and park. The road eventually leads to Loch Lomond which lies at the foot of Mount Bancroft and south of James Peak.

Fall River Road/St. Mary's Glacier

Drive 8.6 miles from the start of the Fall River Road (see above). There is a parking area on the right for St. Mary's Glacier. Across the road from the parking area there is a sign that reads "Glacier Hike." Walk up the rocky jeep road for three quarters of a mile past St. Mary's Lake to the toe of St. Mary's Glacier.

Granby or Grand Lake/Monarch Lake Trailhead

Monarch Lake is the quiet and diminutive eastern annex to the much larger and busier Lake Granby. It sits on the western boundary of the Indian Peaks Wilderness and is the jump off point for several long and beautiful trails that lead eastward through deeply cleft valleys. These valleys culminate in higher alpine basins and cirques at the western foot of the Continental Divide. By Memorial Day, most of the snow has melted from these trails up to about 10,000' enabling ski mountaineers to access some of the most beautiful and remote backcountry to be found anywhere in Colorado.

There are two very different ways to reach Monarch Lake – via I-70 and Berthoud Pass or via Trail Ridge Road. Denverites prefer the I-70 route. Take I-70 west to Hwy. 40 west. Go 46 miles over Berthoud Pass to Granby. At Granby proceed north on Hwy. 34 for five miles to the Arapaho Bay access road (Grand County Route 6). Turn right and drive one mile on a paved road and nine miles on 2WD dirt to the parking area at Monarch Lake. From Denver this route takes roughly two hours to drive.

The more scenic route is to drive over Trail Ridge Road, assuming it has opened. The Park Service tries to have the road cleared and open by Memorial Day. Trail Ridge Road begins in the town of Estes Park. In Estes Park locate Hwy. 34 west, the National Park bypass, and drive five miles to the Park entrance and the start of Trail Ridge Road. Cross the Park, exit the Park, pass Grand Lake and, 9.5 miles from Grand Lake, turn left onto the Arapaho Bay access road described in the preceding paragraph. This route takes about three and a half hours from Denver, or longer if you stop for elk.

Some people hate to remove their skis no matter what.

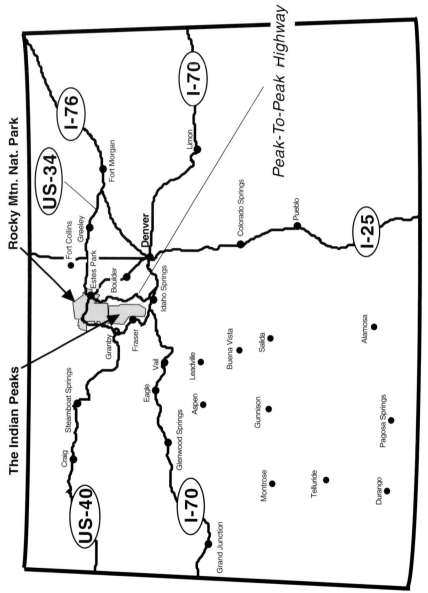

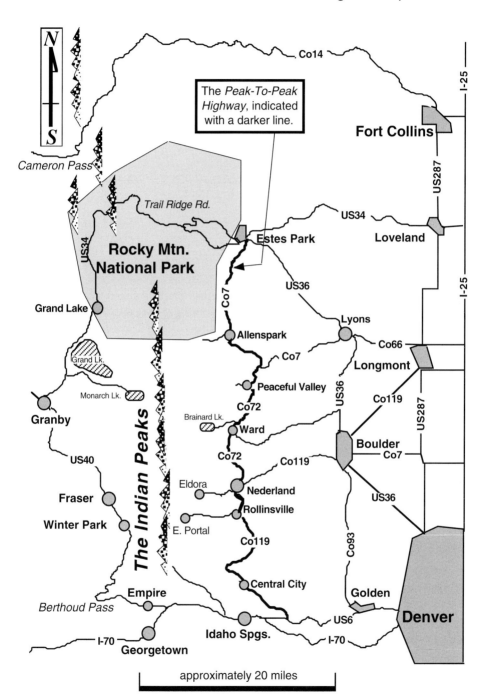

The *Peak-To-Peak Highway*, indicated with a darker line.

approximately 20 miles

REGION 1

Middle St. Vrain Creek and St. Vrain Glaciers

The towering cliffs, glacial cirques and peaks that enclose the head-waters of Middle St. Vrain Creek stand apart from any other region of the Indian Peaks. No other valley in the Indian Peaks demonstrates the power of glaciation as vividly as this one does. The upper valley contains six pocket glaciers, seven summits above 12,000 feet, eight lakes near or above timberline, and a complex series of major creeks and tributaries. The north side of the canyon consists of a nearly unbroken, five miles long escarpment that resists penetration as it rises more than a thousand feet above the valley floor. Carved out of this impressive wall of rock are innumerable overhangs, buttresses, and pinnacles some of which are large enough to be misconstrued as separate summits.

Despite its outstanding natural features, this region sees far fewer visitors than the Brainard Lake region which lies one valley system to the south. The more remote peaks and hanging valleys of Middle St. Vrain are virtually untouched. With the exceptions of St. Vrain and Sawtooth Mountains, which are readily accessible, none of the other peaks is climbed very often. In fact, few backcountry travelers venture beyond Red Deer Lake or Lake Gibraltar.

Crowning the head of the valley stands Ogalalla Peak (13,138') and its easily recognizable neighbor, Elk Tooth (12,848'). Both of these peaks offer excellent steep ski descents. For skiers who prefer more moderate terrain (that includes the option for advanced or even expert skiing) the St. Vrain Glacier Tour offers a strenuous but less intimidating way to log lots of vertical feet of skiing in magnificent surroundings.

Except for Sawtooth Mountain, which can be ascended and descended easily in a day, we recommend strongly that skiers and snowboarders planning to visit the upper portion of the valley backpack into a basecamp at or near snowline and complete the route of their choice during the following day. This recommendation is based on the assumption (which is usually correct) that both of the very rough 4WD roads that lead up to the Wilderness boundary are impassable or closed. If by chance either of the roads is open and negotiable, four to five miles can be cut from the approach, and the routes described can be done in one long day.

Ogalalla Peak and the upper Saint Vrain drainage. "Ogalalla Express" is the wide-topped couloir that lies to the left of the summit.

OGALALLA PEAK (13,138')

Starting Elevation .. 9,180'
Elevation Gain .... 3,960'
Distance .... 19 miles
U.S.G.S. Maps .... Allenspark; Isolation Peak; Ward
Access Point .... Ward/Beaver Reservoir
Best Month .... June
Map .... Page 128
Rating .... Advanced

Ogalalla stands at the head of Middle St. Vrain Creek. Because of its distance from major trailheads, Ogalalla is among the more obscure thirteeners and sees only a handful of visitors each summer. Skiers and snowboarders who are willing to make the long trek to the summit are rewarded with outstanding views of Rocky Mountain National Park, the northern Indian Peaks, and several remote peaks and valleys located west of the Divide. The steep southeast face of Ogalalla is interrupted in only one place by a wide and steep couloir ("Ogalalla Express") that leads to a ridgetop only minutes from the summit. In June one can ascend the mountain by this couloir and then turn around and ski almost continuously to a base camp at timberline for a vertical descent of nearly 2,000 feet.

As suggested earlier in the regional description, skiers should plan on spending one or two nights at a base camp at or below the snowline which in early June is generally above 10,500'. From such a base camp, the summit lies three miles to the west. By camping on the north side of the main creek, crossing the swollen creek can be avoided completely. Further up the valley above timberline, the creek is usually solidly bridged with snow and crossing back and forth is not a problem.

Ogalalla Express - Advanced

Leave camp early and head west keeping to the north side of the creek. Timberline is reached at 10,700' and the valley opens up. Slant to the south side of the snowcovered creek and continue west around the south shore of a small lake at 10,910'. Proceed northwest through a narrows, then up a steep slope to a flat area, and up another steep slope to the uppermost basin, which is actually a depression. To the left is the northernmost St. Vrain Glacier. To the right is Ogalalla Express, the wide couloir that leads to the summit ridge. Climb the couloir 1,200 vertical feet to its top, drop your skis, and amble 0.2 mile over the rocky tundra to the summit.

The top of the couloir approaches 45 degrees and is prone to sluffing as the sun warms the top layer. Ski back down to the basin. Consider ascending and descending all or part of North St. Vrain Glacier or simply ski back to base camp. During the return a short detour to the southeast starting at 11,000' will bring you to the scenic Gibraltar Lakes and views of the southern St. Vrain Glaciers.

"Ogalalla Express." Ogalalla Peak is just outside the right edge of the photograph.

ELK TOOTH (12,848')

Starting Elevation .. 9,180'
Elevation Gain .... 3,670'
Distance .... 17 miles
U.S.G.S. Maps .... Allenspark; Isolation Peak; Ward
Access Point .... Ward/Beaver Reservoir
Best Month .... June
Map .... Page 128
Rating .... Advanced

Elk Tooth is possibly the oddest looking summit in the Indian Peaks. The signature crag that juts out of the mountain is indeed tooth-shaped. However, it is debateable whether or not any known elk has even one tooth that is so canine in shape. In spite of this misnomer, Elk Tooth is an impressive mountain. Its sheer south face rises two thousand feet above the valley floor.

The Snake - Advanced

The eastern edge of Elk Tooth's south face is interrupted by a wide couloir ("The Snake") that is similar in aspect and appearance to the one described previously for Ogalalla Peak. Unlike the couloir on Ogalalla, however, the one on Elk Tooth does not put one as close to the summit. Instead, after reaching the top of the couloir, the summit is still nearly a half mile of scrambling to the west. Despite this fact an ascent and descent of The Snake is challenging and enjoyable. From the top of The Snake there is an excellent view of massive Mount Copeland (13,176') and the lake studded valley of Cony Creek.

To reach The Snake follow the approach route described previously for Ogalalla Peak as far as timberline at 10,700' at which point the valley opens wide. The Snake is the obvious couloir on your right (northwest). Study the couloir and plan your ascent from below. Depending on the locations of runnels, rock outcroppings, and slide debris, you will probably end up snaking back and forth to reach the top. About halfway up the couloir another steeper and narrower couloir branches to the west. This couloir usually has a deep runnel that provides a handy excuse for not attempting it. The top of The Snake provides a range of steepness with the west side being the steepest (45 degrees) and the east side less steep (35 degrees).

Having successfully descended The Snake, consider taking a short tour across the valley to the Gibraltar Lakes. The northfacing glaciers above the lakes are perfect for some post-lunch or pre-siesta skiing on a variety of terrain.

"The Snake" from the south. Elk Tooth is the massive crag that extends out of the upper left corner of the picture.

"The Snake." Skiing in magnificent surroundings

Saint Vrain Glaciers Tour (12,400')

Starting Elevation .. 10,400' (basecamp)
Elevation Gain .... 3,000'-4,000' (total from basecamp)
Distance .... 9 miles (total tour from basecamp)
U.S.G.S. Map .... Allenspark; Isolation Peak; Ward
Access Point .... Ward/Beaver Reservoir
Best Month .... June
Map .... Page 128
Rating .... Advanced

    The far west end of Middle St. Vrain Creek contains six pocket glaciers which face north and hold skiable snow for most of the summer. In June, when the snow in the lower portions of the valley has melted, there is still enough snow near and above timberline to connect four of the six glaciers into a ski adventure that promises between 3,000 and 4,000 vertical feet of superb downhill skiing, straightforward routefinding, and gorgeous scenery. To make it easier to follow the route description that follows, we have chosen to number the glaciers from one to six with one being the northernmost glacier below Ogalalla Peak and six the small glacier that lies south of Envy Lake. During this tour you will ascend and descend glaciers 1,2,5, and 6. It isn't necessary to commit to all four glaciers to complete the tour since any one of them may be omitted. However, inclusion in the St. Vrain Glacier Hall of Fame requires that you complete the suggested route.

    To start the tour from a basecamp below timberline, follow the directions to the uppermost basin below Ogalalla's southeast face. (See Ogalalla Peak). From the base of the upper bowl climb as far as you wish up Glacier #1, turn around and descend. Climb east out of the unusual depression that forms the base of the upper bowl and ski down 300 vertical feet to the east before turning to the south and climbing up into the narrow bowl that holds Glacier #2. Ascend and descend Glacier #2 back down to elevation 11,400. Turn east and continue skiing 400 vertical feet down to and past the narrows and the tiny lake at 10,910. Once past the tiny lake, curve south and uphill to the Gibraltar Lakes. Ascend and descend Glacier #5 and retreat to the north side of the largest Gibraltar Lake. Turn east and head for an obvious low saddle that divides Gibraltar Lake from Envy Lake. Ski 200+ vertical feet to Envy Lake. Turn south and climb and descend Glacier #6 before returning to Envy Lake. Bushwhack around the west shore of Envy Lake and ski down to the north into Middle St. Vrain Creek. Return to camp and dinner.

*St. Vrain Glacier
#2. Point 12,945'
is on the right.*

*Engaged in the
physically demanding
task of orienteering
along the St. Vrain
Glaciers Tour*

*St. Vrain Glacier #5.
Lake Gibralter is in the foreground.
The narrow couloir extending above
the glacier has a cornice and usually
develops a deep runnel.*

St. Vrain Mountain (12,162')

Starting Elevation .. 8,680'
Elevation Gain .... 3,482'
Distance .... 8 miles
U.S.G.S. Map .... Allenspark
Access Point .... Allenspark
Best Months .... April, May
Map .... Page 129
Rating .... Intermediate or Advanced

St. Vrain Mountain is a delightful and relatively short destination that offers solitude, and breathtaking summit views. It makes a fine early season trip while waiting for the snow to stabilize on other higher and steeper routes. The peak can be approached via the official St. Vrain Mountain Trail and the Meadow Mountain bowl or via the Rock Creek route described below. Of course, a loop is another possibility.

From the parking spot on the northwest side of Rock Creek, ski or walk three miles up the road. At 10,200' (the unsigned Wilderness boundary) the road turns sharply to the left (south). Continue straight ahead for 50 yards then turn right (west) and up through steep timber with Rock Creek never more than a couple hundred feet to your right. Try to interconnect a series of small narrow clearings. Eventually the route breaks out into a large clearing. Ascend this clearing and veer slightly north. You've reached the last of the big timber. The head of Rock Creek is a wide, low angled expanse of dwarf spruce. Soon the east ridge (one of the ski descent routes) of St. Vrain Mountain appears. As you ski or walk up this ridge outstanding views of the north faces of Audubon, Paiute, and Sawtooth will supply a needed distraction as well as inspiration for future outings. When you tire of the view south and west, turn your head northward for views of Longs Peak and its brethren peaks rimming beautiful Wild Basin in Rocky Mountain National Park.

The modest summit affords additional generous views of the Middle St. Vrain drainage, the St. Vrain Glaciers, and Wild Basin. Alternatively, the homesick skier can gaze eastward toward the foothills and the high plains, visibility permitting.

East Ridge - Intermediate

This descent requires no explanation. It is short enough to allow multiple descents. Keep in mind that the longer you delay your descent, the sloppier the snow will be especially within the steep timbered area. Take care not to ski over the fragile vegetation on the return.

South Slope- Advanced

Early arrivers in search of a more demanding route may elect to ski the longer and steeper south face down to timberline, slog back up, then ski the northeast face in similar fashion before heading back down. The wide south face holds one major and two minor ski routes. These are steeper than the southeast ridge route, about thirty degrees, hence the advanced rating. The main route starts a few hundred feet west of the summit. Despite its southerly orientation this snowfield lasts through May and into June.

South slope of St. Vrain Mountain. "Red Deer Mountain" is in the background.

Red Deer Lake and "Red Deer Mountain" (12,391')

Starting Elevation .. 8,638'
Elevation Gain .... 3,753'
Distance .... 14 miles
U.S.G.S. Maps .... Allenspark; Isolation Peak
Access Point .... Peaceful Valley/Camp Dick
Best Month .... May
Map .... Page 130
Rating .... Intermediate

Red Deer Lake is a popular destination during the snowfree months of summer and fall. Before then it sees few visitors. The lake, which is at 10,372', is set in a peculiar pocket several hundred feet above the main trunk of Middle St. Vrain Creek. The mountain which we've named "Red Deer Mountain" is the unnamed summit west of the lake. Red Deer Mountain's steep southeast face forms the northern boundary of Buchanan Pass and is taller than its better-known neighbor to the south, Sawtooth Mountain (12,304'). In this respect our giving it a name is justified. The eastern slope of Red Deer Mountain holds snow through May and allows for a nearly continuous ski from the summit to the lake. The downhill skiing from the lake back down to Middle St. Vrain Creek consists of marginal tree bashing.

The route to the lake and the mountain is long. However, in May, about two-thirds of the jeep road from Camp Dick to the trailhead at 9,583' is snow free and can be hiked in and out at a brisk pace. Park at Camp Dick and hike as far as possible before switching to skis. Use skins for the rest of the approach unless the snow is firm enough to walk on. Cross the bridge at 9,583' and continue up the valley past the Wilderness boundary at 9,800'. One mile past the boundary, at the end of a large clearing that has standing dead timber, there is a bridge and a sign for the Buchanan Pass Trail (9,920'). Cross the bridge, ski northwest about 100 yards to where the Buchanan Pass Trail cuts sharply south. Follow the trail cut for another 100 yards, leave the trail, and cut up through the steep timbered slope that separates the trail from Red Deer Lake. Use a map and compass to orient toward the lake. The lake is surrounded by sparse timber making it easy to spot. Continue around the northeast shore of the lake and pause above the outlet. This is a good place for munching and rehydrating and especially for studying the terrain to the west that leads onto the east slope of Red Deer Mountain. You will need to do some zigging and zagging to reach the summit snowfield and finally the summit which is just over a mile away. Incidentally, the summit affords an outstanding view of the skiable snowslope on Sawtooth Mountain.

When the snow on Red Deer Mountain is in top form, you can descend almost 2,000 vertical feet back down to the lake. To return to the Middle St. Vrain road you simply reverse your approach route. In the event that you miss the bridge at 9,920', you should be able to cross the creek on a snow bridge somewhere else and then pick up the main trail nearby.

Backpacking along the Buchanan Pass Trail. The trail passes through a meadow filled with wildflowers. "Red Deer Mountain" is on the right, and Sawtooth Mountain is on the left.

Sawtooth Mountain (12,304')

Starting Elevation .. 9,160'
Elevation Gain .... 3,144'
Distance .... 12 miles
U.S.G.S. Maps .... Allenspark; Ward
Access Point .... Ward/Beaver Reservoir
Best Months .... May/June
Map .... Page 130
Rating .... Advanced

Sawtooth Mountain is one of the most recognizable of the Indian Peaks. One of the best places to view Sawtooth Mountain is from the Peak-to-Peak Highway a few miles south of Peaceful Valley. It is also clearly visible from eastern Boulder County. Its sheer south face and arcing north ridge account for its distinctive sawtooth shape. The northeast face of Sawtooth holds a gem of a snow slope that lasts well into June and is seldom skied. (This is not the snowslope that is usually seen from the above vantage points. The slope usually seen is on the southeast face.) While the summit is some distance from the trailhead, most of the route is a gentle grade. The summit provides closeup views of the northernmost Indian Peaks and Rocky Mountain National Park.

The most direct route to Sawtooth begins on the north end of Beaver Reservoir where a rough and wet 4-WD road leads east 3.5 miles to the Coney Flats Trailhead at 9,780'. The 4WD road rises gently through a cool forest of mixed aspen and conifers. At 3.5 miles the road crosses Coney Creek and ends in a large clearing with views to the west. The start of the Beaver Creek Trail and the Wilderness Boundary are 150 yards further west. Continue west through open meadows and scrub along the Beaver Creek Trail which may be partially snow covered. Should you lose the trail, head for a high, wide and obvious drift of snow that forms annually at around 10,200'. Surmount this drift and dead reckon (the trail is likely to be buried in snow) toward the wide valley that leads to Buchanan Pass. Once on the north side of Sawtooth at an elevation of 10,800' turn to the southwest and climb the snowslope for 1,400 vertical feet to the flat summit ridge. The summit is a few steps to the south.

The descent is extremely enjoyable and only seldom exceeds 30 degrees. The return retraces the approach.

The descent route on Sawtooth Mountain viewed from the northeast along the Buchanan Pass Trail. Only a portion of the descent route below the summit is visible when approaching from Coney Flats.

REGION 2

Brainard Lake

Brainard Lake is the epicenter for ski and snowboard mountaineering in the Indian Peaks. Standing on the bridge at the lake's outlet at 10,300', it is easy to see why. One can't help dreaming of spending a week at the campground and skiing every route in sight. The area's only drawback is the number of hikers, very few of whom travel beyond Lake Isabelle or Blue Lake. By taking advantage of the early-season road closure and by starting out early in the day, you stand a good chance of setting first tracks on the peak of your choice. Caches of good skiing can be found into July. We have skied Mount Toll from the summit to the shore of Blue Lake on July 4, after a good snow year.

From June 1, through September 15, overnight camping is prohibited in the Four Lakes Travel Zone which encompasses Long, Isabelle, Mitchell, and Blue lakes. Camping in the Peak Travel Zone west of these lakes is permitted but is heavily restricted due to the fragility of the tundra and the scarcity of sites. We recommend staying at the rustic Pawnee Campground near Brainard Lake. On weekends arrive early at the campground to find a site since it fills up quickly.

The view west toward the "Grand Cirque" from Lake Isabelle. This is probably the most photographed scene in the Indian Peaks. This photograph was taken in June. The triangular peak on the left is Navajo. The second summit to the right of Navajo is Apache. The large, craggy peak to the right of Apache is Shoshoni, which appears higher than the rest only because it is closer to the camera.

MOUNT AUDUBON (13,223')

Audubon's huge bulk makes it an easy mountain to spot. Its broad gently sloping eastern flank is contrasted by considerably steeper northwest and south faces. The well cairned standard route to the summit is popular during all seasons.

At the Mitchell Lake Trailhead parking area, be sure to locate the Audubon Trail, which is on the north side of the parking circle, and not the Mitchell Lake Trail. The Audubon Trail climbs through timber and quickly reaches a narrow clearing (10,820') with a view to the west and a steep snow slope directly in front. Here the trail cuts sharply right (east) angling up and switchbacking twice before reaching a mellower grade. From here the trail gracefully swings north then west over tundra and rock before reaching a saddle at 12,600'. From the saddle, rock hop south 0.5 mile to the obvious summit.

The view to the north includes the Longs Peak massif, Wild Basin, St. Vrain Mountain, and the peaks around St. Vrain Glaciers. The range to the northwest is the Never Summer Mountains. To the south lie the other Indian Peaks accessible from Brainard Lake. Neighboring Paiute and Toll are close at hand.

East Snowfield

Starting Elevation .. 10,480'
Elevation Gain .... 2,743'
Distance .... 7 miles (to and from summit)
U.S.G.S. Map .... Ward
Access Point .... Ward/Brainard Lake
Best Months .... May or June
Map .... Page 131
Rating .... Intermediate

Skiers may choose to forgo the rocky summit and just ski the big snow patch that lies south of the trail between 12,400' and 11,600'. This is a beautiful place to practice turning in a high alpine setting. Instead of the Mt. Audubon Trail, a more direct approach to this snowfield is as follows: From the 10,820' clearing mentioned earlier, battle directly up the steep snow slope for 200 vertical feet to much flatter ground. Head northwest toward the East Snowfield. This shortcut should be used only when the steep snow slope is stable. Return from the East Snowfield via the nearby Audubon trail.

Crooked Couloir - Advanced

Starting Elevation .. 10,480'
Elevation Gain .... 2,743'
Distance.................. 6 miles (to and from summit)
U.S.G.S. Map .... Ward
Access Point........... Ward/Brainard Lake
Best Months .... June
Map .... Page 131
Rating .... Expert

Crooked Couloir is located on the south face of Audubon. It is a terrific line – long, steep, and seldom skied. It is overshadowed by the ski descent on Mount Toll which usurps most of the area's skiing action. This shallow couloir only comes into view along the Blue Lake trail, 0.5 miles east of Blue Lake. It rises more than 1600 vertical feet above the north shore of Blue Lake.

This couloir can be reached two ways. From the summit of Audubon walk west along the narrow west ridge for about 200 yards. In May and early June the snow in the couloir extends to the ridge top with just enough bare ground to adjust boots and gather up one's courage. The skiing starts out at a reasonable 35 degrees, but steepens noticeably about one-third of the way down. Two thirds of the way down, the grade relents. Cruise the last few hundred yards to Blue Lake.

"Crooked Couloir" on Audubon's south face seen from the vicinity of Blue Lake

The second, more direct approach to this couloir is to take the snow covered Mitchell Lake Trail (same parking area as before) one mile past Mitchell Lake and another easy mile to Blue Lake. Walk around to the north side of the lake and climb the low angle snow at the base of the couloir. At the point where the snow steepens, you may elect to abandon the snow for the talus on the left (west) side of the couloir. If you have summit fever, the top is an obvious 200 yards of talus to the east.

Crooked Couloir faces south, and so an early start is recommended. It melts out by the end of June.

Coney Couloirs - Advanced

Starting Elevation .. 10,480'
Elevation Gain .... 4,143' (summit plus couloir)
Distance .... 8 miles
U.S.G.S. Map .... Ward
Access Point .... Ward/Brainard Lake
Best Months .... June
Map .... Page 131
Rating .... Expert

The three Coney Couloirs are embedded in the steep northwest face of Mount Audubon. They are only visible from the Coney Lakes that lie below or from the higher Indian Peak summits to the north. Viewed from these northern summits the couloirs appear nearly vertical, and no one in his or her right mind would consider making a descent. But as is so often the case, the couloirs are far more moderate than they appear (they seldom exceed 35 degrees). In reality the Coney Couloirs are among the best descents in the Indian Peaks.

The westernmost couloir is the longest and steepest and ends just south of the outlet of Upper Coney Lake. The entrance to the couloir lies at the flat area 250 yards west of the summit. The bottom one-fourth of this couloir may be melted out later in June. When it is in prime condition, one can ski 1,800 vertical feet. The top of the couloir approaches 40 degrees.

The central couloir, whose top is difficult to access and is frequently melted out, lies just below and to the east of the summit. This couloir is not recommended unless approached from below.

The easternmost couloir begins at 12,600' just 50 yards northeast of the point where the Mount Audubon Trail curves to the southwest before beginning the final ascent of the summit cone. The top 100-200 feet of this couloir may be melted out by mid-June. The same is true for the bottom. The steepness hovers around 35 degrees.

Persons wishing to ski any of the Coney Couloirs have two options. The first is to start at the Brainard Lake/Mount Audubon Trailhead, hike up the Mount Audubon Trail, and drop into one of the couloirs from near the summit. To return one climbs back up to the Mount Audubon Trail before returning to Brainard Lake. This is not as ridiculous as it seems and is the least complicated and shortest of the two options. The talus slopes adjacent to the couloirs can, for the most part, be climbed by those who find this preferable to kicking steps up the couloir.

The second option, which makes for a full and rewarding day is to park one vehicle to use as a shuttle at the Ward/Beaver Reservoir access point and to use the Mount Audubon Trailhead near Brainard Lake as a starting point. After hiking the Mount Audubon Trail to one of the couloirs, descend the couloir and return to the shuttle vehicle via Coney Creek and the Coney Creek 4WD Road. By this route the total distance is around ten miles and involves tricky routefinding and bushwhacking. Persons electing this route should familiarize themselves beforehand with the route to the Coney Lakes from the Coney Flats Trailhead. Be advised that above 10,500' the Coney Lakes valley is floored with an impenetrable mat of dense scrub. The south side of the valley below the couloirs is passable by careful routefinding over talus slopes and small snowfields.

The three Coney Couloirs on the northwest face of Mount Audubon. The view is from a point north of the lower Coney Lake. The summit of Audubon is just left of center.

PAIUTE PEAK (13,088')

Starting Elevation .. 10,480'
Elevation Gain .... 2,608'
Distance .... 7 miles
U.S.G.S. Maps .... Ward; Monarch Lake
Access Point .... Ward/Brainard Lake
Best Month .... June
Map .... Page 131
Rating .... Advanced

Like many of the Indian Peaks, Paiute is a mountain of contrasts. Viewed from Coney Lake the northeast face of Paiute presents a 2,000 foot high obstacle to climbers. This face of Paiute is dark and forbidding. From Blue Lake, however, the south side of Paiute appears sunny, climbable, and especially skiable. Tucked as it is between massive Audubon to the east and Toll to the south, Paiute is usually climbed or skied as an afterthought. There are skiers and snowboarders who ski Toll annually and only eventually get around to investigating Paiute. Similarly, Paiute is often climbed after Audubon via a connecting ridge. Take time to investigate this delightful thirteener.

The most obvious descent route on Paiute is the south facing run we call "Curvaceous Couloir." The couloir is visible from the plains east of Boulder, if you know where to look for it. From Blue Lake and the alpine lake at 11,833', the couloir is easy to spot. It is used for the ascent to the summit as well as the descent. Since it faces south an early start is required to avoid wallowing in knee-deep slush on the descent. Noon is too late for a descent!

To reach Paiute drive to the Mitchell Lake Trailhead near Brainard Lake. Travel the mostly snowcovered trail past Mitchell Lake and continue past some ponds to Blue Lake. The snowcovered trail is difficult to follow because the valley is a patchwork of meadows, rock outcroppings, and impassable dwarf spruce. Avoid skiing over or through the fragile vegetation. Close attention to your map should help. (Hiking this trail in late summer and noting key landmarks will help with navigation when the trail is snowcovered.)

Rest at Blue Lake and marvel at the mind-boggling scenery and descent routes. Visible from left to right are Mount Toll, Curvaceous Couloir, and Crooked Couloir on Mt. Audubon. To reach the base of Curvaceous Couloir, ski to the north side of Blue Lake and ascend north and west along ledgy terrain to the unnamed lake perched at 11,833'. Locate the base of the couloir a bit higher and further west and ascend it. If time allows, avoid the temptation to ski the couloir immediately, and ascend the south ridge to the summit of Paiute. Careful planning on the way up will enable you to ski 1,500 vertical feet down to Blue Lake.

"Curvaceous Couloir" on Paiute Peak. This view is from Blue Lake.

MOUNT TOLL (12,979')

Starting Elevation .. 10,480'
Elevation Gain .... 2,499'
Distance .... 7 miles
U.S.G.S. Maps .... Ward; Monarch Lake
Access Point .... Ward/Brainard Lake
Best Months .... June/July
Map .... Page 131
Rating .... Expert

Conjure up an image of the ideal ski descent. It would be esthetic, long, challenging, originate at a summit, and be surrounded by beautiful and rugged scenery. This is a perfect description of Mount Toll. Like its neighbors, Paiute and Audubon, Toll is clearly discernible from points east of Boulder. Travelers in and around Boulder County can monitor its snow condition as summer progresses. Toll is closely watched and frequently skied. For many it is an annual ritual. The route faces south and sees many visitors – two reasons to get an especially early start from the trailhead.

Standing at the east end of Blue Lake and looking up at the snow covered southeast face, one cannot avoid facing the fact that Toll's midsection is steep. One consolation is that the top of the route is much gentler and allows a chance to make a dozen or so warm-up turns before committing to the serious section. Another is that the west edge of the snowy face is slightly less steep. In June it is usually possible to ski continuously from a point just below the summit to the west shore of Blue Lake, a total of 1,600 vertical feet. Another dubious bonus is that on most weekends a crowd of spectators at Blue Lake will be analyzing and discussing your technique.

Mount Toll is reached by hiking or skiing from the Mitchell Lake Trailhead near Brainard Lake. (Follow the directions described previously for Paiute Peak.) After a rest at Blue Lake, hike south and west around the lake onto a series of snow ramps intermixed with patches of talus. These ramps lead west into the base of the small cirque ("Toll Bowl") between Pawnee Peak and Toll. Head steeply west up the headwall to the saddle between these peaks, turn north and climb to the summit. Easily visible from the summit are the surrounding Indian Peaks as well as the peaks and side valleys of upper Cascade Creek. There is also an impressive view of Fair Glacier west of Apache Peak. A few steps back down bring you to the start of the descent. With views this great you'll be in no rush to start your descent.

Mount Toll from the east. Blue Lake is in the foreground.

The descent does not retrace the ascent route. Instead, after exiting the steepest part of the face, start curving to the east and then northeast on fairly wide slopes and flats that lead to the west end of Blue Lake. Return via the south side of the lake. Make note of this lower half of the route before starting your climb up from Blue Lake.

Ascending Toll in June

PAWNEE PEAK (12,943')

Starting Elevation .. 10,500'
Elevation Gain .... 2,443'
Distance .... 7.2 miles
U.S.G.S. Maps .... Monarch Lake; Ward
Access Point .... Ward/Brainard Lake
Best Months .... May/June
Map .... Page 132
Rating .... Intermediate or Advanced

Unlike its neighbors to the north and south, Pawnee Peak is a difficult mountain to spot from the plains or from Brainard Lake where only a bit of its summit is visible. The best view of the peak and its snowy southeast slope is from the Brainard Lake Road roughly a mile before reaching the lake. More easily identified is Pawnee Pass, which is south of the peak and accessible by a trail. This pass is an important route for crossing the Continental Divide from east to west into the remote valleys that dissect the western slope of the Indian Peaks.

In addition to the obvious (and short) intermediate snowfield that stretches from the summit and down the southeast slope of Pawnee Peak, there are several varied descents in the vicinity of the peak which make a trip to Pawnee worthwhile. The summit can be skied from late April until mid-June. The steeper routes ("The Keyholes") below the summit snowfield should only be skied later in the season (usually June) when the snow has consolidated.

Southeast Slope - Intermediate

This is a route that you will want to ski, reclimb, and ski again. It is high, wide, and skiable from the summit. To reach Pawnee Peak, start at the Long Lake Trailhead near Brainard Lake, assuming that the Brainard Lake Road has opened (usually by June). If the road isn't open, park at the winter closure near Red Rock Lake and walk or bicycle the three miles to the trailhead. This is an easy and scenic walk that adds about an hour at each end of your day. From the trailhead, walk or ski 0.25 mile to Long Lake, pass Long Lake and continue up to Lake Isabelle, two miles from the trailhead. Lake Isabelle is an extremely popular Indian Peak destination – a fact requiring no explanation.

A sign near the east end of the lake points the way to the Pawnee Pass Trail which heads north and then west 0.75 mile into a small, rocky, and obscure basin due east of Pawnee Pass. (The trail from Lake Isabelle is incorrectly marked on the U.S.G.S. Monarch Lake quadrangle.) At the west end of this basin, admire the three steep rock-walled couloirs, The Keyholes, with a tiny pond (11,320') at the foot of the rightmost couloir. If you would like to attempt one of them on the return, make careful note of their locations with respect to the surroundings.

From the little basin angle up and southwest to gain the flat spot (11,800') on the ridge that juts southeasterly from Pawnee Pass. Climb steeply up this ridge to Pawnee Pass. The big cirque that stretches between Pawnee Pass and Shoshoni Peak is "Shoshoni Bowl." The peaklet (12,878') south of the pass is "Pawshoni" and is another excellent descent (see below) that can be combined with Pawnee Peak. From the broad area of the pass the route north to the summit is obvious.

Ski the southeast slope of Pawnee and retrace your steps back to the flat spot at 11,800'. The slope from the pass to this flat spot can be skied. Alternatives are to climb and ski "Pawshoni" and then, perhaps, one of the Keyholes which makes for a lot of turns without a tremendous effort.

Pawnee Peak and the gentle Southeast Slope descent route are on the right of the photograph. The second "Keyhole" is on the left of the photo and the third "Keyhole" is to the left of center.

The Keyholes - Advanced

The Keyholes are steep couloirs that drop due east of Pawnee Pass into the little basin described above in the approach to Pawnee Peak. Combined with the Southeast Slope route, it is often possible in early June to ski from the summit, down one of the couloirs, and down the drainage to the east end of Lake Isabelle, a vertical descent of 2,300'. The first (left) couloir and the middle couloir are the longest and steepest. The third (right) couloir is shorter and is only steep at its very top. The middle couloir melts out and exposes rocks sooner than the others. It is not recommended.

Shoshoni Bowl - Advanced

The broad cirque ("Shoshoni Bowl") between Pawnee Pass and Shoshoni Peak is obvious during the ascent of Pawnee. Shoshoni Bowl can be skied a variety of ways. The central portion tends to melt out first but the bowl's north and south sides hold snow into June and provide a variety of skiing terrain. The bottom of the cirque funnels into a steep, rocky gully that opens onto the west end of Lake Isabelle. This is not a safe way to exit the bowl. The preferred exit is to walk north to the Pawnee Pass Trail.

"Pawshoni" 12,878' - Advanced

"Pawshoni" lies just south of Pawnee Pass and makes a great addition to a descent of Pawnee Peak. It is a short climb from the pass to the summit of Pawshoni. From the summit there is a view of Pawnee Lake on the west side of the Divide. One can ski directly east from the summit to the base of Shoshoni Bowl (see above), have some refreshments, and then ascend a short distance to the Keyholes for a dramatic final descent. Regardless of one's choice, the return route is only a few hundred yards to the north.

North Face - Advanced

For those who prefer to make a circuit route out of a trip to Pawnee, this is a variation which isn't done very often. From the summit walk a few hundred feet to the west and drop down (north) to the obvious snowslope that leads into the bowl ("Toll Bowl") between Mt. Toll and Pawnee Peak. Continue skiing to the west shore of Blue Lake as described above for Mt. Toll. Return via Blue and Mitchell Lakes and the Mitchell Lake Trail. The Mitchell Lake Trailhead is a short walk from the Long Lake Trailhead.

Skiing an intermediate route in June. Perfect sky – perfect snow

SHOSHONI PEAK (12,967')

Starting Elevation .. 10,500'
Elevation Gain .... 2,467'
Distance .... 10 miles
U.S.G.S. Maps .... Monarch Lake; Ward
Access Point .... Ward/Brainard Lake
Best Months .... May or June
Map .... Page 132
Rating .... Advanced

Isabellitis – noun. A common disorder of the neck that afflicts visitors to Lake Isabelle. Caused by incessant craning of the neck toward the incredible panorama of Navajo, Apache, and Shoshoni Peaks that lie to the west of the lake.

The grand cirque that is bounded by Navajo, Apache, and Shoshoni Peaks is the signature landform of the Indian Peaks, reproduced on countless postcards and calendars. The cirque holds two permanent snowfields, Navajo Snowfield and Isabelle Glacier as well as several couloirs that may be skied into July. This area draws mountain lovers of all persuasions like a magnet. And yet, we have skied these peaks on June weekends and been all alone. The key to finding solitude in this area is, as always, an early start.

North Face - Advanced

Shoshoni's north face is still another good ski descent that may be accessed from the Pawnee Pass Trail. The run originates near the summit and drops almost 1,000 vertical feet to the base of the bowl on the north side of Shoshoni Peak. To reach the base of the north face, follow directions along the Pawnee Pass Trail (see "Pawnee Peak") to the flat area at 11,800' and then head directly toward the face which can be climbed to a point at or near the summit. Cornices are not a problem.

Shot In The Corner Pocket - Advanced

There is an obscure couloir that leads up to the plateau, 300 yards west of Shoshoni's summit. It originates at the northeast corner of Isabelle Glacier. It is most easily spotted by noting where the rock walls around the corner of the glacier form a right angle. It starts to melt out by the middle of June and has a cornice which deserves respect.

Follow the directions to reach Lake Isabelle (see "Pawnee Peak"). Keep on the trail along the north shore of the lake and continue west for a mile to an unnamed lake at 11,420'. Climb the snow slope at the west end of this lake to flatter ground at 11,900'. (You'll ski down this slope on the return.) Turn north and rock hop over the moraine that bounds the south side of Isabelle Glacier. Locate the "Shot", climb it, summit Shoshoni, and ski 700 vertical feet down to Isabelle Glacier.

If time permits, consider a descent of Apache and/or Navajo Snowfield described in later sections. A descent of all three – Shot In The Corner Pocket, Queen's Way or Apache Couloir, and Navajo Snowfield – will entitle you to bragging rights back at the parking area.

The north face of Mount Shoshoni. The summit is right of center.

APACHE PEAK (13,441')

Starting Elevation .. **10,500'**
Elevation Gain .... **2,941'**
Distance .... **8.5 miles**
U.S.G.S. Maps .... **Monarch Lake; Ward**
Access Point .... **Ward/Brainard Lake**
Best months .... **June and July**
Map .... **Page 132**
Rating .... **Advanced or Expert**

As the second highest Indian Peak and with steep slopes on all sides, Apache looms large when viewed from all points of the compass. Any attempt to ski Apache should include a trip to the summit. The view is tremendous. There are views of the intricate north face of North Arapaho, rarely-seen Triangle Lake below Fair Glacier, and the entire Cascade Creek drainage to the northwest.

Clearly visible from Brainard Lake are two couloirs that attract climbers and skiers once the snow has consolidated. Both of these couloirs hold snow through July and snow lingers in their lower portions through the summer. But unlike a good wine, as the snow ages it becomes less mellow as icy patches, rough spots, footsteps, and grit accumulate. For maximum enjoyment ski these in June or early July.

To reach the base of Apache from Brainard Lake follow directions to Isabelle Glacier as described under Shoshoni Peak.

Queen's Way - Advanced

This snowy ramp is a steep extension of Isabelle Glacier. It is located along the south edge of the small northeast face of Apache. It does not extend, as one would hope, to the summit of Apache.

From the southwest corner of the glacier, climb the ramp to its top. Here the summit is hidden from view. To reach the summit traverse over mixed snow and boulders 300-400 yards southwest to the summit. Reverse your route for the descent. Depending on conditions, it may be possible to ski as far as the west end of Lake Isabelle.

Apache Couloir - Expert

This couloir appears as a mirror-image of Queen's Way when Apache is viewed from the east. It is steeper and more intimidating than Queen's Way. It too leads to a point a few hundred yards from the summit. Early in the season, the top of the couloir blends into a large, lower angled snow field that allows you to crank lots of "practice" turns before dropping into the couloir.

To reach Apache Couloir follow directions to Isabelle Glacier. Instead of turning north toward the glacier, turn southwest toward Navajo Snowfield. Apache Couloir is on the right near the base of Navajo Snowfield. Climb it and the gentler slopes above it to the south ridge which can be followed 200-300 yards to the summit. Reverse your route for the descent. Energetic skiers may elect to ascend and ski Navajo Snowfield before pointing their skis toward Brainard Lake.

Apache Couloir is a popular ascent and descent route for people climbing Apache especially during summer weekends. The couloir, which faces east, catches early morning sun. For these two reasons plan on an especially early start and keep an eye out for others in the couloir.

Late July. Skiing into the "throat" of Apache Couloir

NAVAJO PEAK (13,409')

Starting Elevation .. 10,500'
Elevation Gain .... 2,600 (to top of Navajo Snowfield)
Distance.................. 8.5 miles
U.S.G.S. Maps .... Monarch Lake; Ward
Access Point........... Ward/Brainard Lake
Best Months............ June and July
Map .... Page 132
Rating...................... Expert

Navajo Peak is the alpine culmination of Niwot Ridge, the huge ridge that stretches seven miles from the Peak-To-Peak Highway to the Continental Divide. Niwot Ridge is the site of the University of Colorado's renowned Mountain Research Station. The climate, flora, and fauna of the ridgetop resemble those found at arctic latitudes making Niwot Ridge an excellent site for studying alpine environments.

Navajo is a distinctive cone with a large, steep snowfield on its north side. Unlike most of the other Indian Peaks, there is no "walk up" route to the summit. The easiest route which is close to a walk up but which involves a bit of scrambling near the top is "Airplane Gully", a class 3 route. Unfortunately, the Airplane Gully route is 0.3 mile east of Navajo Snowfield. The route to the summit from the top of Navajo Snowfield is Class 4. (Anyone wishing to combine an ascent of Navajo Peak with an ascent and descent of the snowfield should consult Gerry Roach's guidebook which is listed in the Appendix to this book.)

A curious feature of Navajo is the easily recognized, 75 foot pinnacle jutting from the ridge between Navajo and Apache. Its name is "Dicker's Peck."(hmmm) It's only usefulness, aside from titillating the mountaineer's sophomoric imagination, is that it serves as a handy gauge of one's progress up the snowfield, for when you've reached Dicker's Peck, you've reached the top!

To reach Navajo Snowfield follow directions to the base of Apache Couloir (see Apache Peak.) That's where Navajo Snowfield is. If you're lucky, some fellow climbers will have already kicked steps up the snowfield. The top of the snowfield is at 13,100'. The view south into Wheeler Basin is dizzying. This is the best place to study the north face of North Arapaho. Take a moment to contemplate a ski descent of this face (described later).

Now back to Navajo Snowfield. The descent is steep, sustained and extremely satisfying. As with the other descents in the grand cirque, it is usually possible to ski to the west end of Lake Isabelle, a vertical drop of 2,200'.

A rocketing glissade down Navajo Snowfield demonstrates the awesome combination of gravity and a low coefficient of friction.

REGION 3

Middle Boulder Creek

The streams and valleys that feed Middle Boulder Creek comprise the most extensive watershed in the Indian Peaks Wilderness. This watershed stretches from South Arapaho Peak to Rollins Pass. It is in this region that we find the greatest number of ski descents. Many of the approaches are long and elevation gains from the Hessie Trailhead are 1000 feet greater than trips originating at Brainard Lake. Long glacially carved valleys lead upward to secluded basins. Many of the descent routes aren't visible until one is a mile or less from the route. For all of these reasons many fine descents are seldom skied. Very few people have heard of "Challenger Glacier," "Devil's Thumb Mountain," or the "Elevator Shaft" on "Skyscraper Peak".

Overnight wilderness camping is easier to find in this region. In addition there is limited car camping at the Buckingham Campground at the Fourth of July Trailhead. One can find supplies, groceries, permits, and restaurants in the nearby town of Nederland which is only 25 minutes from downtown Boulder.

"Yee-Haa!" On "Devil's Thumb Mountain." The distant summit is James Peak.

The remote North Face of North Arapaho Peak

NORTH ARAPAHO PEAK (13,502')

Starting Elevation .. 10,130'
Elevation Gain .... 3,372'
Distance .... 16 miles
U.S.G.S. Maps .... Monarch Lake; East Portal
Access Point .... Nederland/Fourth of July Trailhead
Best Months .... June/July
Map .... Page 133
Rating .... Expert

Anyone who has summited Navajo Peak or Apache Peak undoubtedly has been struck by the magnificent, snow-streaked north face of North Arapaho which lies two miles to the south. North Arapaho is the highest of the Indian Peaks. In conjunction with South Arapaho Peak, it forms one of the most recognizable massifs along the Front Range especially when viewed from the city of Boulder and east Boulder County.

In his guidebook, Colorado's *Indian Peaks Wilderness Area*, Gerry Roach introduces the north face by stating, "This has to be the most obscure route in the Indian Peaks Wilderness. No matter how it is done, the approach is long and arduous." And we certainly concur! Anyone planning to ski the north face should be prepared to spend two days out and is advised to ascend at least to the top of the Navajo snowfield to study the complex series of couloirs of the face.

The north face is located on the west side of the Divide above the upper reach of Wheeler Basin, itself an obscure and seldom-traveled valley. Wheeler Basin is a side branch of Arapaho Creek which forms a beautiful forested canyon stretching from Caribou Lake (11,147') near the Divide to Monarch Lake over a distance of seven miles. You have the option of reaching Wheeler Basin via the Arapaho Creek Trail, which originates at Monarch Lake, or via the Fourth of July Trailhead and the Arapaho Pass Trail on the east side of the Divide. We suggest the latter route.

From the Fourth of July Trailhead hike along the gently graded Arapaho Pass Trail to the popular summit of Arapaho Pass (11,906'). From the Pass, the trail turns briefly north before beginning a series of downhill switchbacks into the Caribou Lake basin. At the first switchback stop and use your map to identify Coyote Park, a large clearing in the valley directly to the north. Leave the trail and make an angling descent slightly east of north along snowfields into the thinly forested area which eventually opens into Coyote Park. Camp overnight along the east edge of Coyote Park at about elevation 10,360. Because of the length of the return route from the north face back to the trailhead, a pre-dawn start is suggested for the second day of the trip. Another possibility, of course is to spend two nights at Coyote Park.

To reach Wheeler Basin from Coyote Park head north along the east edge of the Park and aim for a timbered bench above elevation 10,480'. A gradual ascent will deposit you on the flatter (but still quite rugged) south side of Wheeler Basin clear of the steep, cliffy terrain that lies to the west. Angle northeasterly until you reach the creek. There is a good trail (which may be snowcovered) on the north side of the creek. Reaching this involves an easy but wet crossing of Wheeler Creek at around 10,500'. Whether or not you cross the creek, battle your way along the drainage for a half mile at which point the basin opens into an astonishingly beautiful high valley. At the last moment the north face will come into view.

Study the face and the approach carefully. The two best ski routes lie on the right (west) side of the face. While neither of the two actually extends to the summit itself, they both reach the northwest ridge. The closest one can get to the summit is to climb the couloir that leads to a U-shaped platform at the base of a prominent pillar. From the platform turn left (southeast) along a lower angled snow ramp that leads to the top of the northwest ridge (13,040'). Scramble a quarter mile to the broad summit or forgo the summit and descend along the ascent route.

When snow is plentiful on the face and in the bowl, one can earn 2,000 vertical feet of skiing. All the couloirs and snowfields on the north face reach 45 degrees and should be skied cautiously.

The north face of North Arapaho viewed from Wheeler Basin

SOUTH ARAPAHO PEAK (13,397')

Starting Elevation .. 10,130'
Elevation Gain .... 3,267'
Distance................... 4.5 miles
U.S.G.S. Maps .... Monarch Lake; East Portal
Access Point .... Nederland/Fourth of July Trailhead
Best Months .... June/July
Map .... Page 133
Rating .... Expert

The "Skywalker" couloir on the south face of South Arapaho is one of the most accessible and most exciting Indian Peak descents. When viewed from the Fourth of July mine site, the couloir appears to be an intimidating prospect for a descent. The top of the couloir pushes 50 degrees. The route is often used as a technical alternative to the Glacier Trail route for climbing South Arapaho. The condition and amount of snow in the couloir varies from year to year especially near the ever-steepening top of the route. We suggest that the route be studied, ideally with binoculars, before attempting a descent. We recommend that a climbing helmet be worn while in the couloir due to the inset nature of the route and the potential for rockfall.

The top half of the couloir is bounded on the east by a rock wall that shades the couloir until mid morning. For this reason the snow in the couloir, which faces south, does not experience the softening effects of the sun until later in the morning. This should be taken into account when timing your approach, since starting out too early will make ascending the couloir dangerous when the snow is hard unless you choose to wear crampons. This is one of the few exceptions to the "get an early start" rule. An involuntary glissade down this couloir poses two risks: first is the risk of bodily injury; second is the risk of humiliation since your descent will be witnessed by the hordes headed for Arapaho Pass.

To reach Skywalker, hike from the Fourth of July trailhead toward Arapaho Pass. At the obvious Fourth of July mine site (1.5 miles from the start), turn north along the signed Arapaho Glacier Trail for about 100 yards. Turn off the trail and head directly toward the couloir. Climb the couloir to the top. At this point a decision must be made whether to climb to the summit. The most sensible route to the summit ridge is to exit left (west) near the top of Skywalker and enter a steep, narrow couloir. At the top of this slot, follow the talus north a short distance to the summit ridge. The summit lies 100 yards to the east. This route is a questionable undertaking unless one is suitably equipped and experienced. Alternatively you may choose to forgo the summit and ski the couloir directly. The total descent is between 1000 and 1500 vertical feet depending on how high you climb and on how much snow has melted along the runout of the couloir.

The "Skywalker" couloir embedded in the south face of South Arapaho

CARIBOU MOUNTAIN (12,310')

Starting Elevation .. **9,980'**
Elevation Gain .... **2,330'**
Distance .... **7.5 miles from Caribou**
U.S.G.S. Map .... **Nederland; Ward**
Access Point .... **Nederland/Caribou**
Best Months .... **April, May, June**
Map .... **Page 134**
Rating .... **Intermediate or Advanced**

Caribou is one of several eastern subpeaks of the sprawling Arapaho Peaks. The Arapaho Peaks and the Arapaho Glacier are familiar landmarks to residents of Boulder County. The broad east ridge of South Arapaho culminates at the gentle summit of Caribou. The large stone summit cairn is visible from the end of Caribou Road #128, which is one of two possible access points. The view north from the summit into the lake strewn, forked drainage of North Boulder Creek ranks among the finest in the Indian Peaks. Sadly this drainage and the snowy slopes that nourish the dozen lakes below are off limits to recreationists since the lakes are part of the City of Boulder Watershed (see information about the Watershed in the Introduction). So for now be content to enjoy the scenery and the skiing that is legal. There are two enjoyable routes on Caribou that differ markedly from each other.

East Slopes - Intermediate

The wide open slopes that lie east and slightly south of the summit are ideal for carving dozens of turns on 2,000 vertical feet of low angled snow. This is a good early season route when boggy Caribou Park is still snowcovered. Careful routefinding is necessary since the shortest path is, for the most part, off trail. From the car-park at the beginning of jeep road 505, take some time to study the terrain to the north and to identify Caribou by its huge cairn. Pinpoint the landmarks on your map.

Ski directly north off-trail and drop 150 feet into Caribou Park. From Caribou Park continue slightly west of north aiming for the faint timbered saddle that lies on the west side of Pomeroy Mountain. At the crest of the saddle aim downhill for the point on the map where Horseshoe Creek enters a swampy meadow. Ski across the meadow and locate an old tote road that runs northwest paralleling the meadow's edge. Ski west on this road as it continues on the north side of the unnamed tributary of Horseshoe Creek. At around 10,000' the track disappears once steeper terrain is encountered. Continue up the drainage to timberline. From here the route to the summit is an obvious and pleasant slog. To return simply reverse the approach.

Tuckerman's Two - Advanced

Eastern skiers who once cut their backcountry skiing teeth in New Hampshire's Tuckerman's Ravine can indulge in a bit of nostalgia on the east side of Caribou. Tuckerman's Two bears a striking resemblance to its namesake in the White Mountains. At first steep and technical for 600 vertical feet, the route ends in a gentle cruise back to the lakes.

From the Rainbow Lakes Campground, head west on the Rainbow Lakes Trail which passes along the north sides of the lakes. Once past the last Rainbow Lake continue west-northwest into the bowl. Ascend the bowl and continue to the summit of Caribou for outstanding views and a lunch stop before taking the plunge.

right: Skiing the east slope of Caribou Mountain
below: "Tuckerman's Two" from Rainbow Lakes

MOUNT NEVA (12,814')

Starting Elevation .. 10,130'
Elevation Gain .... 2,684'
Distance................ . 7.5 miles
U.S.G.S. Maps .... Monarch Lake; East Portal
Access Point .... Nederland/Fourth of July Trailhead
Best Months .... June/July/August
Map .... Page 135
Rating .... Advanced & Expert

Mount Neva is a prominent, easily recognizable peak located a mile southwest of Arapaho Pass. Because of its accessibility and its proximity to the pass and lovely Lake Dorothy, it is climbed often. The short, wide bowl at the base of its northeast face is fairly steep. Above the bowl there are several steep couloirs (40+ degrees). It is possible to ski from the summit, down one of these couloirs, down the bowl and out onto flatter terrain at 11,500' east of the peak - a total of 1,300 vertical feet. There are other possibilities such as the short, esthetic couloir at the east end of the bowl; yo-yoing up and down the bowl (also relatively short); or playing on the strange corniced snow drift improbably located at the base of the bowl. Whatever your mood, plan on spending some time around the peak and around Lake Dorothy as well. Your car is an easy 3.5 miles away.

Mount Neva is a snap to get to. From the Fourth of July Trailhead, hike three miles west to Arapaho Pass along the well-maintained Arapaho Pass Trail. At the pass the trail continues west on flat tundra 0.3 mile to Lake Dorothy, a large alpine lake in a beautiful setting. Rock hop around the east shore of the lake and pick your way toward the center of the snow bowl below Neva. This is a good place to ponder your options. There are four obvious couloirs that empty into the bowl. These are described from east to west (left to right). The eastmost couloir is short, wide, and picturesque and has no cornice. The next couloir is known as "Juliet." It also has no cornice, but its top is quite steep (50 degrees). The next one, "Desdemona," has a truck-sized, overhanging cornice topping its right side. It is as steep as Juliet, and is obviously less safe. At the north end of the bowl is a wider couloir known as "Phoebe." It is a bit longer than the others and has a more benign cornice above its left side. The cornice is avoidable by keeping to the right as you look up. With the exception of the first couloir, they all lead to the summit ridge, the summit being a short, pleasant walk away. The summit provides great views of the Arapaho Peaks, the back sides of Arikaree, Navajo, Apache and the peaks surrounding Lone

Eagle Cirque. As usual Long's Peak looms in the distance. The two unnamed lakes to the south comprise the headwaters of the North Fork of Middle Boulder Creek.

A word of caution is necessary. When ascending the couloirs, stay at least six feet away from their rock walls. The moats that form during spring and summer may be deep enough to swallow a climber in his or her entirety.

Having skied the route of your choice, you can exit the bowl one of two ways. Either return back to Lake Dorothy and the Arapaho Pass Trail or ski down and out of the bowl from its east side to the boggy flat area east of the Pass. If you choose the latter, turn northeast when you reach the flats, cross alternating talus, tundra, and snowfields for 0.25 mile, then turn north and uphill to reach the Arapaho Pass Trail.

North face of Mount Neva viewed from Lake Dorothy

"JASPER PEAK" (12,923')

Starting Elevation .. 10,130'
Elevation Gain .... 2,793'
Distance................. 8.5 miles
U.S.G.S. Maps .... Monarch Lake; East Portal
Access Point........... Nederland/Fourth of July Trailhead
Best Month .... June
Map .... Page 135
Rating .... Expert

"Jasper Peak" is the next major mountain south from Mount Neva along the Continental Divide. From its summit, there is a fine ski descent called "Snow Lion" that plunges steeply down the southeast cirque that lies above Upper Diamond Lake. From the bridge crossing of Middle Boulder Creek (see below), the route is mostly a snow-covered trail and routefinding to Upper Diamond Lake and beyond to Snow Lion is not difficult.

Jasper's southeast cirque is a compact, steep-walled feature that holds several steep couloirs that lead directly or close to the summit. Snow Lion is a relatively short but steep couloir that splits the center of the cirque and tops out within feet of the summit. Its steepest section, which is short, approaches 45 degrees. There is no cornice at its top although a large cornice lurks to the climber's right. Because it faces east, it should be climbed and skied early in the day. Portions of the route may be roughened by previous sloughing and cornice breakage from neighboring gullies.

From the Fourth of July Trailhead, follow the Arapaho Pass Trail one mile uphill to the signed junction with the Diamond Lake Trail. Descend the Diamond Lake Trail 0.5 mile to the bridge crossing of Middle Boulder Creek. (The Diamond Lake Trail has been rerouted west and north of the purple trail shown on the East Portal map.) The south bank of Middle Boulder Creek is generally snow-covered in May and early June. As a result, following the trail (one mile) to Diamond Lake requires vigilance. Keep a compass handy in case the trail eludes you. The Diamond Lakes are set in a long, broad-mouthed hanging valley which is hard to miss. When you reach the lake try to stay high on a snow-covered bluff north of the lake. The flat terrain north and west of the lake is marshy, willowy, and spongy and should be avoided. Stay north of the main drainage, and, map in hand, look around for a mostly snow-covered high route that leads upvalley. Pass just south of an unnamed small lake at 11,350', then bee-line for the outlet of Upper Diamond Lake. Travel along the north side of the lake and into the southeast cirque. Snow Lion should be obvious, topping out just right of the summit. From the lower Diamond Lake to the Upper Lake is 1.5 miles; from the Upper Lake to the summit is 0.75 mile.

As you enter the cirque and begin your ascent, beware of the huge overhanging cornice east of Snow Lion. Ascend Snow Lion directly, reveling in your proximity to the summit when you kick your last step. From the summit you can check out snow conditions on James Peak and "Devil's Thumb Mountain" to the south. Mount Neva, the Arapaho Peaks, Navajo, Apache and others are visible to the north. In the distance is Long's Peak. When your eyes are full, return to the top of Snow Lion and ponder your first turn. Having descended the couloir, aim your skis or snowboard for Upper Diamond Lake and enjoy the ride. Ski past the beautiful lake on its south side this time. With a good snowpack and advance planning, you can catch a few more skiable pitches down to about 10,800' and below Diamond Lake – 2,000 vertical feet in all. Recross the bridge and bask in the sunshine on the north side of the creek. Don't forget to stop to admire the June wildflowers, especially the blue columbine and Indian paintbrush.

East Face of "Jasper Peak" above Upper Diamond Lake. "Snow Lion" starts at the right of the summit. The summit is the second highest snowy point in the photograph.

"Devil's Thumb Mountain" (12,650')

Starting Elevation .. 9,000'
Elevation Gain .... 3,650'
Distance .... 14 miles
U.S.G.S. Maps .... Nederland; East Portal
Access Point .... Nederland/Hessie
Best Month .... May
Map .... Page 135
Rating .... Intermediate (Advanced option)

While there is a "Devil's Thumb" on the East Portal map, there is no official "Devil's Thumb Mountain." The high point on the Divide, due west of Storm Lake, and north of the mountain that spawned the Devil's Thumb pinnacle on its southeast side is what we call "Devil's Thumb Mountain." The peaklet itself is only visible from Storm Lake. But the Jasper Lake and Storm Lake basins (where the skiing is) can be spotted on the trip in.

This is a long and demanding trip that offers routefinding, great scenery, solitude and 1,800 vertical feet of downhill action. An especially early start is suggested. The majority of the route follows the trail to Jasper Reservoir (a.k.a. "Lake."). Since most of this route will be snow covered in late April and May, close attention to your map and to the landscape is essential.

At the Hessie Trailhead, cross the big footbridge and hike up the broad, winding path to higher ground. A few feet before the next big wooden bridge and on your right you'll see a trail and sign to Jasper Reservoir. This is the summer trail. While it may be passable and snow-free in sections, we prefer the more obvious route straight ahead. Pass the signed left turnoff to Lost Lake at the edge of a clearing. From this clearing, two valleys are obvious to the west. The valley to the left is the broad valley that leads to King Lake; the equally broad right valley is that of Jasper Creek, your destination. Keep an eye on this valley during the next few miles. Continue past the signed King Lake Trail turnoff just after another bridge crossing. Hike straight across the large meadow, past the Wilderness boundary, for about a mile until you reach the Devil's Thumb/Woodland Lake Trails junction. Turn right across a primitive bridge. This is the only reasonable way to cross the flooded creek. Take careful note of your route from here in order to find the bridge on the way back. (Remember that shallow ski tracks are shortlived under the intense spring sun.) Follow the right (northeast) bank of Jasper Creek up a steep section. As the terrain levels off, try to locate the trail which slants gradually up toward Jasper

Lake. This "trail" is actually an old road that was used to access the Jasper reservoir dam. For this reason it is easy to locate. In places the trail disappears under deep snow drifts.

Once on the trail again, avoid the temptation to veer upslope to the north on inviting snow ramps. These will place you on a scenic bench 200 feet above the lake and make you feel dumb! (We can attest to this.) Consult your map often. From the outlet of Jasper Reservoir, the rest of the route is easy to find. Ski around the west bank of the lake to the inlet that descends from Storm Lake above. Ski up this streambed to Storm Lake's outlet. Ski around the north bank of Storm Lake and eye the wide descent route to the west as well as the conical peaklet (Devil's Thumb Mountain) to the right of the descent route. Huff 'n puff up the slope to a windblown flat area, turn northward and climb the steep, snowy east ridge of the gorgeous peaklet. Watch the surrounding mountains emerge – James Peak to the south, Neva, "Jasper Peak," and the Arapaho Peaks to the north and northeast. After you've had enough alpine scenery, descend the peaklet and ski and smile down to Jasper Lake.

"Devil's Thumb Mountain" from Lower Storm Lake

"CHALLENGER GLACIER" (12,120')

Starting Elevation .. 9,000'
Elevation Gain .... 3,120'
Distance .... 14 miles
U.S.G.S. Maps .... East Portal; Nederland
Access Point .... Nederland/Hessie
Best Months .... June/July
Map .... Page 136
Rating .... Expert

Challenger Glacier is one of the steepest descents in the Indian Peaks. The uppermost portion of the slope, which is separated from the cornice above by a crevasse, reaches 50 degrees. The condition of the snow, which may be roughened by debris from broken cornices and wet sloughs, and the large cornice should be studied carefully before climbing and skiing this route. Like most of the steeper routes in this book, the lower portion of the route is more user friendly. The snowfilled bowl at the base of the glacier is a fine place for intermediates to play between bouts of sunbathing. Neither Challenger Glacier nor its sister glacier to the south, "Skyscraper Glacier," are drawn on the U.S.G.S. East Portal map.

In June the long hike up to the Challenger Glacier area is delightful. The route begins at the vacated townsite of Hessie. From the Hessie Trailhead cross the bridge and follow the winding path uphill to the next bridge. A few feet before this bridge there is a sign on the right for Jasper Reservoir. This is the start of the Devil's Thumb bypass trail. This trail is not shown on the U.S.G.S. East Portal map but is shown on the *Trails Illustrated* map that covers the Indian Peaks.

In June, when it is free of snow, the Devil's Thumb bypass trail provides a more direct and scenic route up the valley than does the main trail which continues straight ahead across the bridge. Steep at first, the bypass trail crosses large meadows before eventually climbing into the Jasper Creek drainage. From here the trail follows an old road that slants gradually up the hillside on the north side of the valley, and eventually reaches the outlet of Jasper Reservoir about five miles from Hessie. Avoid the temptation to stop for lunch at the reservoir. Instead continue about a mile further along the trail to beautiful Devil's Thumb Lake located at timberline. This is a great place to refuel and to survey the surrounding bowls. Challenger Glacier is in view to the southwest. It is set in a northeast-facing pocket due west of "Skyscraper Peak" (12,383').

The inconspicuous summit of "Skyscraper Peak" lies to the south. Other fine ski descents can be seen as well.

The easiest way to reach the Challenger Glacier bowl is to continue along the trail to Devil's Thumb Pass. The trail to the pass shown on the U.S.G.S. map has been rerouted to the south where it now accesses the Divide via the spur just southwest of the tarn at 11,250'. Where the trail starts to climb the spur, leave the trail and hike south cross-country into the bowl at the foot of the glacier. The route is obvious from here.

If the glacier is not in a skiable condition, two other routes may be more appealing. Both lie north of the glacier. The first is a narrow ramp and the second is a broader, more typical bowl. For those wishing to ascend Skyscraper Peak, there is a snow and scree-filled gully to the south that leads to a point just east of the summit. Be advised that climbing down into Challenger Glacier from the Divide is a dicey undertaking.

"Challenger Glacier" viewed from "Skyscraper Peak." The pitch just below the cornice approaches 50 degrees.

"ELEVATOR SHAFT" (11,800')

Starting Elevation .. 9,000'
Elevation Gain .... 2,800'
Distance .... 11.5 miles
U.S.G.S. Maps .... Nederland; East Portal
Access Point .... Nederland/Hessie
Best Month .... June
Map .... Page 136
Rating .... Advanced

This relatively unknown, funnel-shaped couloir is located on the north side of the long east ridge of "Skyscraper Peak" (12,383'). ("Skyscraper Peak" is a prominent but unnamed summit northwest of Skyscraper Reservoir. See the next description for more details.) The "Elevator Shaft" is seen by hundreds of people who pass along the trail to Jasper Reservoir and Devil's Thumb Lake. From this vantage point the route appears to be relatively inaccessible. This is not the case. Despite a somewhat long approach this is an extremely satisfying descent with a beautiful approach that traverses flower-filled meadows and aspen stands with just enough off trail travel to make it interesting.

"Elevator Shaft" viewed from the trail to Jasper Reservoir and Devil's Thumb Lake

Starting at Hessie follow the route described under Challenger Glacier. Having located the Devil's Thumb Bypass Trail, stay on it as it passes through open meadows and crosses into the Indian Peaks Wilderness. At this point there should be no question as to why this area has a federal Wilderness designation. After two miles from the start of the Bypass trail, you'll reach elevation 10,400'. The Elevator Shaft is visible from here. Leave the trail and head due west across patchy snow and sparse timber through an old logging site. Cross to the south bank of the main creek at about elevation 10,500' and aim uphill directly for the base of the Elevator Shaft which is a quarter of a mile to the southwest.

Climb the couloir to where it widens into a snowfield, then angle right (west) to the farthest extension of the snow at about 11,800'. From here there is an excellent view north toward "Jasper Peak" (12,923') and the Storm Lakes - Jasper Reservoir basin. Finally, push the "Down" button and enjoy the descent. The return is identical to the approach.

"SKYSCRAPER BOWL & PEAK" (12,383')

Starting Elevation .. 9,000'
Elevation Gain .... 2,893' to Point 11,893'
                     3,383' to Skyscraper Peak
Distance .... 12 miles
U.S.G.S. Maps .... Nederland; East Portal
Access Point .... Nederland/Hessie
Best Months .... May/June
Map .... Page 136
Rating .... Advanced

      This route leads up one of the Indian Peaks' least visited valleys toward two lovely lakes – Woodland Lake which is subalpine and Skyscraper Reservoir which is alpine. A trip to these lakes is a satisfying experience at any time of the year. If time permits, one can visit nearby "Skyscraper Peak" (12,383').

      Two snow slopes extend above Skyscraper Reservoir. Neither is very long. However, what this route lacks in skiing thrills it makes up for in rugged scenery and solitude. Try to time your visit around the end of May when the average snowline will be around 10,000'. At this time the Woodland Lake Trail will be mostly snowcovered and your descent can be extended by an additional 1,000' vertical feet.

      From Hessie follow the route description for "Devil's Thumb" Mountain. At the Devil's Thumb/Woodland Lake Trails junction turn left heading west initially along the south bank of the creek. If the creek has already melted out, you can follow this steep trail up to the valley of Woodland Lake and then continue along flatter ground to the lake. Early in the season when the creek is still choked with snow it may be easier to ski directly and even more steeply up the creek bed. Following the steep section, the creek flattens noticeably and from here the most open route to the lake can be found roughly fifty yards north of the creek. Continue west-southwest to the lake.

      From the outlet of Woodland Lake survey the upper bowl where Skyscraper Reservoir is located. The best skiing routes are from Point 11,893' down to the reservoir and also on the southeast face of Skyscraper Peak, northwest of the reservoir. The southeast face route is steeper and sits below a cornice. Also note that the south ridge of Skyscraper Peak is blocked by a toothlike buttress which makes it necessary for climbers to use the east ridge or else climb directly up the snowcovered southeast face to a point just east of the summit.

The easiest route to the upper bowl and Point 11,893' is to pass Woodland Lake on the north, ski west 300 yards, then turn southwest to the left of the round knoll which is adjacent to the small dam that plugs the reservoir. Continue on to Point 11,893'. From this summit there are good views of the broad alpine basin that contains Bob, Betty, and King Lakes. Skyscraper Glacier is visible to the north above Bob Lake and Rollins Pass lies south beyond King Lake. To reach the summit of Skyscraper Peak via the southeast face pass the reservoir on its north side and continue west to the base of the southeast face.

Both descent routes can be skied without a huge expenditure of energy. When snow conditions are good the skiing back down to the main trunk trail is a pleasurable contrast with the trudge up to the lakes.

The south face of "Skyscraper Peak" viewed from Woodland Lake

REGION 4

South Boulder Creek and Rollins Pass

This region stretches from Rollins Pass on the north to James Peak on the south. One would never guess that this region is not part of the Indian Peaks Wilderness since it is every bit as wild as regions to the north that are in the Wilderness. The reason that the South Boulder Creek watershed isn't part of the Wilderness is that until 1994 much of it was privately owned. In 1994 the land was sold to the Forest Service. At the time of this writing Wilderness advocates are campaigning for inclusion of this area into the Indian Peaks Wilderness. Let's hope that they prevail.

Peter Bridge

Ascending "Frosty Mountain."We're smilin' thanks to our nifty heel lifts.

In addition to the lengthy main corridor of South Boulder Creek which reaches the north slope of James Peak on the Divide, there are four alpine basins that lie north of South Boulder Creek. Three of these basins, Crater Lakes, Arapaho Lakes, and Forest Lakes, each have ski descent routes and demand solid routefinding skills. The approaches into these basins are not as long as some others further north, but they gain elevation more quickly.

Except for the North Slope route on James Peak, which takes a full day to complete, the rest of the routes in this region can be completed by early or mid-afternoon with an early start. The exception might be "Radiobeacon Mountain" and the Forest Lakes basin where multiple routes can be enjoyed over a two day period. Overnight camping is permitted in this area.

The S. Boulder Creek Region has excellent opportunities for overnight camping.

"SKYSCRAPER GLACIER" (12,160')

Starting Elevation .. 10,711'
Elevation Gain .... 1,450'
Distance .... 9 miles
U.S.G.S. Map .... East Portal
Access Point .... Rollins Pass (via Yankee Doodle Lake)
Best Months .... June and July
Map .... Page 136
Rating .... Expert

Skyscraper Glacier is located at the north end of the large alpine basin that holds Bob, Betty, and King Lakes. It is not identified on the U.S.G.S. *East Portal* map. It is located on the steep slopes northwest of Bob Lake. Its name-sake is nearby "Skyscraper Peak" (12,383'), also unnamed on the *East Portal* map. Short and steep, Skyscraper Glacier can be skied along with other nearby descents without a major expenditure of time or energy. Nearby Skyscraper Peak can be climbed easily by following the west ridge to the knobby summits (there are three). The walk to Skyscraper Glacier and Peak from Rollins Pass via the Corona Trail is heavenly. There are wildflowers in profusion, marmots bustling, and birds calling which contrasts markedly with the rawness and icy sterility of the Divide in winter.

To reach Skyscraper Glacier and Peak, park at Yankee Doodle Lake and follow the directions to Rollins Pass given earlier under "Access Points." (The snowfield above and west of Yankee Doodle Lake may be skied on the return.) From the pass, hike north about two miles along the Corona Trail. When Point 12,307' is directly to your right (east), leave the trail and wander northeast and east toward the higher ground which is Skyscraper Peak. After a quarter mile locate the dropoff and cornice of the glacier on your right. It is unlikely that you will be able (or want) to access the top of the glacier via its corniced top. Instead pass by the top of the glacier and locate a grassy, south-west facing gully that lies along the east edge of the glacier. It is more reason-able to descend this gully a bit and then traverse out onto the middle of the glacier which can be climbed from this point. Consider dropping your gear at the top of the gully, hiking to the nearby summit of Skyscraper, and returning to the glacier.

After skiing the glacier, proceed around the west side of Bob Lake and continue along a terrace that leads past over-camped patches of bare ground by the outlet of Betty Lake. Cross the outlet (wet) and locate the poorly marked trail leading from Betty Lake. Follow it down to the King Lake Trail and ascend the King Lake Trail back to Rollins Pass. The steep slopes west and northwest of King Lake can be skied.

"Skyscraper Glacier" from the southeast. Point 12,307' is to the left of the glacier.

KING LAKE BOWLS & ROLLINS PASS
(12,000')

Starting Elevation .. 10,711'
Elevation Gain .... 1,289'
Distance .... 6.5 miles
U.S.G.S. Map .... East Portal
Access Point .... Rollins Pass (via Yankee Doodle
Lake)
Best Months .... June/July
Map .... Page 136
Rating .... Intermediate or Advanced/Expert

     Its close proximity to Rollins Pass makes King Lake one of the most visited lakes in the Indian Peaks. All this attention is justified since the lake sits in beautiful surroundings below and out of sight of the pass. Proximity to the pass also attracts alpine skiers and snowboarders to the high steep bowls above the lake. The runs here are short but they are steep enough to test one's skills.

The "King Lake Bowls" from the southeast one-half mile east of Rollins Pass. The bowls sit above the high basin containing King, Bob, and Betty Lakes. King Lake, which is out of the picture, is to the left of the leftmost bowl.

King Lake Bowl - Advanced

The two best descents are located in a small cirque above and north-west of King Lake. There is an unnamed sausage-shaped tarn at the base of this cirque. The precise locations of these two runs can be pinpointed during the hike to the pass from the east.

From Rollins Pass, start out heading north on the Corona Trail. After about a mile, veer east to the edge of the tundra and locate the top of either the first or second descent route. Having skied one route, the second can be climbed and skied. To exit, head southeast to a slope that drops down to the north edge of King Lake, cross the outlet, and find the King Lake Trail a few yards from the crossing. Ascend the trail back to Rollins Pass.

Rollins Pass Runs - Intermediate

There are two parallel ski slopes that extend north-northeastward from the east edge of Rollins Pass. They both hold reliable snow through May and June and provide a training ground for skiers who prefer to practice their turns without the commitment of a long approach.

FOREST LAKES BOWL & COULOIRS (11,900')

Starting Elevation ..... 11,010'
Elevation Gain .... 900'
Distance .... approximately 2 miles
U.S.G.S. Map .... East Portal
Access Point .... Rollins Pass (Forest Lakes Trailhead)
Best Month .... June
Map .... Page 137
Rating .... Advanced or Expert

The routes described below can be viewed from the Forest Lakes Trail-head along the Rollins Pass Road. All of them lie within two steep-walled cirques north of Point 12,072' ("Radiobeacon Mountain"). The first bowl lies due west of Point 11,054' on the Rollins Pass Road and drops from the Divide to a tarn. The second bowl is due west of the upper Forest lake and also drops from the Divide to a tarn. The third is, in fact, a couloir set into the northeast face of "Radiobeacon Mountain." This couloir is very steep and narrow, and skiing it is a serious undertaking.

The easiest way to reach the first bowl is to park at the trailhead and walk 0.2 mile north on the road past the ridge on the west side of the road. Turn left off the road and bushwhack up to the north side of the ridge which can be easily ascended on mixed talus and grass. From the top of the ridge hike a short distance to the Divide and then south 0.2 mile to the top of the bowl. Ski the bowl to the tarn at its base. To return to the trailhead ski southwest uphill past a knoll, then ski down into the next bowl at the base of the second and third runs mentioned earlier. There is another tarn here. Pass the tarn on its north side and hike down a steep slope to the upper Forest Lake. The trail back to the trailhead is on the north side of the lake 200 vertical feet below the trailhead.

The second bowl, which is further south, can be reached the same way as the first and by hiking an additional 0.2 mile south along the Divide. However, the presence of a cornice might make an approach from below easier than launching off the cornice. Return as described above.

The couloir on Radiobeacon Mountain can be skied from the top, but because of its steepness and the potential for poor conditions, it is more sen-sible to ascend the couloir before skiing it. It is 800 vertical feet.

"Radiobeacon Mountain" and Forest Lakes bowl and couloirs from the southeast

"RADIOBEACON MOUNTAIN" (12,072')

Starting Elevation .. 9,211'
Elevation Gain .... 2,861'
Distance .... 8 miles
U.S.G.S. Map .... East Portal
Access Point .... Rollinsville/East Portal
Best Months .... May/June
Map .... Page 137
Rating .... Advanced

About a mile and a half before reaching East Portal examine the snowy skyline above the dirt road. The mountain at the extreme right with the broad snow slope originating at the summit and running down its east-northeast face is an unnamed peak dubbed "Radiobeacon Mountain." This mountain is so named because the U.S.G.S. map indicates that there is a radiobeacon on its summit. All that's left of this structure is a 10 foot by 10 foot concrete pad lying a stone's throw from the summit. This modest-looking peak rises above the Forest Lakes and is a gem to ski. The steep-walled cirques that flank the mountain to the north and south create an awesome backdrop and outstanding photo opportunities.

Walk fifty yards toward the tunnel entrance and cross the tracks. Continue on a gravel path and cross the aqueduct on a small bridge. Walk or ski the path along South Boulder Creek past cabins and small clearings. At 0.3 mile a large clearing marks the junction of Arapaho Creek with South Boulder Creek. Continue ahead crossing Arapaho Creek, enter the woods again, and stop when you reach another large clearing marked "Grave" on the map 0.3 mile from the last clearing. Just as you enter the clearing, make a sharp right, advance 150 feet uphill and locate the wide and well-graded pack trail that leads to Forest Lakes. Turn right and ascend this easy trail.

After the trail recrosses Arapaho Creek, it arcs north and northwest through pleasant woods. A large clearing marks the confluence of Arapaho Creek and the creeks from the Forest Lakes. The creeks will likely be snow covered in May. The peak to the northwest with the gently sloping east ridge is Radiobeacon Mountain. The first Forest Lake (situated on the map under the word "Lakes") lies just beyond the east ridge. From the clearing turn northeast and head up a steeper timbered slope. When the terrain flattens noticeably, turn northwest and you should hit the lake (10,660') after 200 yards or so.

Radiobeacon Mountain and the ski descent route will be obvious from the east side of the lake.

Head for the northwest corner of the lake, continue fifty yards up a short steep slope, turn west toward the peak and climb to the base of the east slope. Study the slope for the safest line of ascent. The sparsely timbered knoll-like hump to the right of the slope is a good intermediate destination before committing to the final snow pitch. From the hump climb moderate snow to the summit. The crest of the Divide stretching from James Peak (looking south) to the Arapaho Peaks (looking north) is visible from the summit. Other interesting sights include the Winter Park Ski Area and the Williams Fork Mountains to the east, Fraser Valley to the northwest, Rollins Pass to the north, and the Needle Eye Tunnel along the Rollins Pass Road to the northeast.

The best line of descent begins 100 feet south of the summit, 35 degrees at first but moderating to 25 degrees before a flatter respite. Retrace your ascent route back to the lake, admire your tracks, then slide back to your car. In mid May you should be able to keep your skis on during the entire return trip.

The east slope of "Radiobeacon Mountain" viewed from the dirt road two miles east of East Portal. The partial mountain in the left of the photograph is "Frosty Mountain."

"FROSTY MOUNTAIN" (11,960')

Starting Elevation .. 9,211'
Elevation Gain .... 2,749'
Distance .... 8 miles
U.S.G.S. Map .... East Portal
Access Point .... Rollinsville/East Portal
Best Months .... May/June
Map .... Page 137
Rating .... Intermediate/Advanced

"Frosty Mountain" is essentially a big bump on the Continental Divide, 0.4 mile south of "Radiobeacon Mountain" (described previously). It is neither named nor numbered on the U.S.G.S. map. It sits at the head of the mile wide cirque ("Frosty Bowl") that cradles the Arapaho Lakes. It is easy to spot from the gravel access road one mile west of East Portal, where the road crosses the railroad tracks. Look for a symmetrical, snowcovered pyramid to the left of Radiobeacon Mountain.

Frosty Mountain offers a delightful intermediate descent in a large bowl that otherwise is threatened by steep headwalls and menacing cornices. Except for the final 100 feet below the summit, the descent along the east ridge of the mountain is between 25 and 30 degrees. There is snow on the mountain and in Frosty Bowl through June.

To reach "Frosty" follow directions to Radiobeacon Mountain. When you reach the large clearing that marks the confluence of Arapaho Creek and the creeks from the Forest Lakes, turn sharply left (west, south west) and ascend the moderately steep timbered slope for about 400 vertical feet. Try to locate a swath through the trees that will deposit you a couple of hundred feet north of the pond at 10,780'. Locating this swath will make the descent easier as it is wide enough to make turns.

As the grade eases continue west along a line just south and above Arapaho Creek. Frosty Mountain lies dead ahead. The mountain to the north is Radiobeacon Mountain (12,072'); to the south is "Sprint Peak" (12,110'). Plot a route to the base of Frosty's east ridge and ascend the ridge and final steep section to the summit. Conditions permitting, in early May it should be possible to ski continuously to the East Portal trailhead. There are other obvious lines in Frosty Bowl. Consider climbing and skiing the steep ramp on the south side of Radiobeacon Mountain.

The east slope of "Frosty Mountain." The mountain holds snow well into the summer, and it's easy to envision it smothered with chocolate syrup and chopped nuts (low-fat, of course.)

CRATER LAKES & CRATER LAKES COULOIR* (12,000') (*see photo page 19)

Starting Elevation .. 9,211'
Elevation Gain .... 2,789'
Distance .... 7 miles
U.S.G.S. Map .... East Portal
Access Point .... Rollinsville/East Portal
Best Months .... May/June
Map .... Page 137
Rating .... Advanced

You won't find any majestic summits along the Divide between Sky-scraper Peak and James Peak. On the other hand there is excellent skiing above and around the many lakes that are located in the high basins east of the Divide. The Crater Lakes along with King Lake and the Forest Lakes described earlier exemplify the beauty and challenge of peak-free ski mountaineering.

Don't let the short distance between East Portal and the Crater Lakes lull you into believing that this is a short, fast outing. Reaching the Crater Lakes from the South Boulder Creek trail involves careful routefinding. There are at least three ways to bushwhack from the main drainage up towards the four lakes. We think that the route described below is the most straightforward.

At elevation 9,960' along the South Boulder Creek Trail, leave the trail and climb uphill through the trees along a compass bearing of 315°. Soon you will reach a short but steep rock band at about elevation 10,320'. It is necessary at this point to find a way around this obstacle which stretches to the left and right for long distances with only occasional breaks. Having negotiated the rock band, turn northward toward the outlet stream that drains the southernmost Crater Lake. Be patient and study the terrain carefully at all times during the climb to the outlet stream.

From the outlet stream the route is easy to follow. Follow the stream for 200 yards or so to the twin Crater Lakes. Walk west along the isthmus that separates the two Crater Lakes. Climb the steep snow-covered face west of the lake, then angle right (north) past a knoll to an overlook above the outlet of the upper lake. Drop a short distance to the lake and follow the south shore of the lake into the base of the cirque.

Crater Lake Couloir is readily identifiable in the southwest corner of the cirque. It is capped by a serious cornice that often breaks, spilling debris into the couloir. Climb all or part of the couloir (depending on its condition) and ski back down to the upper lake. Retrace your steps uphill to the aforementioned overlook. From here climb southwest as high as you can to the top of the steep snowslope that lies east of the twin lakes. The run down this slope to the lakes is outstanding. Between the descent of the couloir up in the cirque and the descent above the two lakes, you can log 1,500 vertical feet. To return to East Portal retrace your steps back to the South Boulder Creek Trail.

Above Crater Lake. What climbs up...will ski down.

REGION 5

Fall River

As you drive west on Interstate 70 out of Denver the highway eventually reaches the top of the long grade up Mount Vernon Canyon. At this high point a mesmerizing view of seven peaks from Berthoud Pass to James Peak suddenly pops into view. This is the Fall River Region. Except for James Peak and St. Mary's Glacier at the north end, the other peaks see very little, if any, skiing activity during the spring. This area is better known for its fishing than its skiing. In fact the skiing along these peaks is excellent in May or June. We have stood alone on the summit of Bancroft and Parry and watched as a dozen or more skiers climbed James Peak a couple of miles to the north. If you're looking for solitude, straightforward routefinding, and delightful skiing amid beautiful surroundings you should plan a trip to either Parry Peak, Mount Eva or Mount Bancroft. The paved Fall River Road extends to the St. Mary's Glacier trailhead at 10,500', a real bonus when one is planning to climb and ski 13,300' James Peak, 3000' above the car. Dirt roads branch off the main Fall River Road and lead within a few miles of the other peaks in this region. Within one to three miles from your car, you can find good camping near Loch Lomond, Fall River Reservoir, or Chinn's Lake.

Fall River Region from I-70 west. Eva is in the center and James is on the right.

The seldom seen true summit of Mount Eva. The north face descent route can be seen below and to the left of the summit. The prefered descent on Eva is on her south side. This photograph was taken in early June from a point close to the summit of Parry Peak.

JAMES PEAK (13,294')

Among local skiers, James Peak is well known for a relatively accessible and long ski route on its southeast shoulder. This popular (and crowded) route is approached from St. Mary's Glacier. However, there are three additional ski mountaineering routes on James. One of these (North Slope Route) utilizes an access point other than the St. Mary's Glacier Trailhead and provides a more complete mountaineering experience. The other two can be reached from St. Mary's Glacier or from the remote James Peak Lake Trailhead above Mammoth Gulch. This latter trailhead is higher and shortens the trip distance, but it requires the use of a high-clearance 4WD vehicle. In addition the high, rough road that leads to the James Peak Lake Trailhead may be blocked by snow one or two miles from the trailhead. St. Mary's Glacier or the James Peak Trailhead? - the choice is yours.

North Slope Route

Starting Elevation .. 9,211'
Elevation Gain .... 4,083'
Distance .... 10 miles
U.S.G.S. Maps .... East Portal; Empire
Access Point .... Rollinsville/East Portal
Best Month .... May
Map .... Page 138
Rating: .... Intermediate

This route is located on James' seldom visited, broad north slope. It is definitely less crowded than the East Slopes Route (see below). Starting at East Portal follow the trail along South Boulder Creek. (See "Radiobeacon" Mountain for a description.) When you reach the clearing marked "Grave" on the U.S.G.S. map, continue on the S. Boulder Creek trail as it climbs steadily for a half mile before leveling a bit.

At 10,480' the official trail turns right (west) along the northern branch of S. Boulder Creek. Instead of following this trail which leads to Heart Lake, continue straight on snow along the southern branch of S. Boulder Creek. After a half mile of steepening forest, the grade eases as you step into the sunshine above timberline. Veer slightly left away from the creek bed and aim for the south (left) side of Haystack Mountain.

Continue up into the impressive cornice-rimmed bowl that lies between Haystack on the right and James on the left. Much of the descent route is visible from the tiny emerald tarn that lies in a depression at the base of the cirque. Your choices for ascending are as follows: kick steps up the long snowfield on James' north slope or, if free of snow, amble up the grassy slope to the left of the snowfield. The ascent is steep for the first 600 vertical feet but eventually gives way to a broad, low angle slope. At this point the ease of travel coupled with unfolding views to the west and north will steal your breath more than any previous portion of the hike in.

Walk to the summit or as far up as the snowfield extends. Fraser Valley sits far below to the west. The prominent snowy peak to the west above the town of Fraser is Byers Peak, which incidentally is fun to ski. To the south from east to west are four fourteeners - Evans, Bierstadt and the twin summits of Grays and Torreys.

If you can bear to leave, hop on your boards - or board - and link perfect turns on ego snow. The extra ego will come in handy as you approach the 30 degree finale. Coast past the tarn, make a few more turns, coast some more and keep 'em turning into the forest.

Starlight Couloir

Starting Elevation .. 11,580'
Elevation Gain .... 1,714' (or more depending on snow closure)
Distance .... 4.8 miles (or more depending on snow closure)
U.S.G.S. Map .... Empire
Access Point .... Rollinsville/James Peak Lake Trailhead
Best Month .... June
Map .... Page 138
Rating .... Expert

The majestic east face of James Peak can only be seen closely and in its entirety from the Mammoth Gulch Road. The face is nearly 800 feet high and is penetrated by several very steep, snow-filled couloirs (the "Star" couloirs). These couloirs are documented snow-climbing routes. The more moderate "Starlight" couloir slices through the more north-facing section of the east face, and for this reason, is not visible unless one is standing at the base of the east face or on top of the northeast ridge.

The "Starlight Couloir" on James Peak. This is one of the more obscure routes on an otherwise very popular peak.

Sometime around mid-June, the Mammoth Gulch Road is sufficiently snow-free that you can drive within a mile or two of the airy James Peak Lake Trailhead at 11,580'. This road and trailhead are one of the more scenic starts to an outing. Standing at the trailhead one's inclination is to walk a mile downhill to James Peak Lake, climb up to the base of the east face, locate the "Starlight" couloir, climb it and ski it. This is certainly an option. However, we suggest the following circuit route which takes advantage of the trailhead's high elevation and also offers great views.

From the trailhead hike uphill cross-country in a south-southwesterly direction to 12,000' and attain the northern edge of the mile-wide east shoulder of James Peak. Turn west, drop a bit passing point 11,887', then continue west toward the northern edge of the east slopes where the east face drops off. Upon reaching 12,800' on the east ridge, the next step is to locate the top of the couloir which is only 20 feet wide at its top, faces north, has no cornice, and is walled in by rock. You must be standing at the top of it looking down to see it. The solution is to inspect every couloir you pass. If a couloir looks as though you would need a rappel to get into it, it is not the right couloir! The top of "Starlight" is located at around 12,930' and the very top may be melted out or icy. A few feet of easy scrambling down is needed to reach the snow.

Once you've located the couloir, you may drop your skis to mark the couloir and head the rest of the 0.3 mile to the summit. Or you can just ski the couloir and forget the summit. The maximum steepness is 40 degrees and it widens fairly soon. The vertical drop into the east face basin is 700 feet. Watch out for rocks that have fallen into the couloir from the adjacent rock walls. Consider wearing a climbing helmet. If after seeing the couloir, you decide that it is too intimidating to ski, relax. There are some kinder, gentler slopes farther back along the ridge that lead either into the bowl below the east face or down toward James Peak Lake. One of these (*"Bailout"*) is described below.

Having successfully descended the couloir, ski north along the base of the east face and then arc northeast onto the southeast side of the northeast ridge. (Are these compass directions making you crazy?) This route allows relatively easy, snow-free access to James Peak Lake. But if you want more skiing, pass 50 yards south of the tiny 11,800' depression which is the bowl's low point. Boulder hop east across the moraine until you see an opening onto the wide snow slope that rises above the west side of the lake. Ski down to the edge of the lake and locate the tiny cabin that sits above the lake's outlet. Hike around the south shore of the lake to the cabin. The trail back to the trailhead begins at the cabin. Portions may be snowcovered, but it is generally easy to follow. The trailhead is a mile from the lake and 400 feet above the trail's low point at 11,180'.

Bailout

Starting Elevation .. 10,380'
Elevation Gain .... 2,740'
Distance .... 8.0 miles
U.S.G.S. Map .... Empire
Access Point .... Fall River Road/St. Mary's Glacier
Best Months .... May/June
Map .... Page 138
Rating .... Advanced

This route can be accessed via either the St. Mary Glacier or James Peak Lake Trailheads. The preferred start is at St. Mary's Glacier. Follow the description for the southeast slopes route given below. Once on the east ridge you can see the top of the route. Hug the edge of the east ridge, and once you've passed the 12,800' top of the steeper section, the ridge flattens noticeably and Bailout is visible on your right. Continue a bit further uphill to the top of the snow slope. This is the start of Bailout.

Bailout is a lovely line that curves down 1,900' vertical feet to the south shore of James Peak Lake. The easiest exit is to climb the steep, talused slope that lies east of the descent route back to the broad plateau at 11,280'. Hang a left (east) and return to the glacier and your car.

Southeast Slopes

Starting Elevation .. 10,380'
Elevation Gain .... 2,914'
Distance .... 8.0 miles
U.S.G.S. Map .... Empire
Access Point .... Fall River Road/St. Mary's Glacier
Best Month .... May
Map .... Page 138
Rating .... Intermediate

The southeast slopes route is the route most commonly skied from the summit of James Peak. When snow conditions are good (late April and May), it is a popular route among skiers of all abilities. The lower portion is pleasantly angled and is a beautiful place for budding skiers and snowboarders to sharpen their turning skills. The short, south-facing drop from the summit has enough steepness to push intermediate skiers.

From the St. Mary's Glacier trailhead walk up the steep, rocky and/or snow covered jeep road to St. Mary's Lake. Turn north from the lake and walk a short distance to the glacier. Foot and ski tracks abound. Walk or ski up the glacier to the immense, flat, and often wet east ridge of James Peak. Stroll westward to obvious steeper ground and follow the southeast ridge to the summit. The descent is as obvious as the ascent. The summit provides closeup views to the south of Bancroft, Parry and Eva. All of these peaks have fine ski descents. The view to the north extends to Rocky Mountain National Park.

The run from the summit to the flat area is a mile long and 1,300 vertical feet. After skiing down to the flat area, there is an additional 400 vertical feet of skiing down St. Mary's Glacier. There is a variety of ways to descend the glacier.

The southeast slopes and east ridge of James Peak. The east face is partially visible with the summit directly above the face. "Bailout" is the slope that drops off to the right in front of the east face.

Mt. Bancroft (13,250')

Starting Elevation .. 10,400' (varies)
Elevation Gain .... 2,850'
Distance................... 6.5 miles
U.S.G.S. Map .... Empire
Access Point........... Fall River Road/Alice
Best Months .... May/June
Map .... Page 138
Rating...................... Intermediate or Advanced

Some of the loveliest alpine descents in the Indian Peaks can be found from Mount Bancroft south to Mount Witter. Mount Bancroft is the first mountain south of James Peak. Overshadowed by the sprawling mass of James Peak, Bancroft and its southerly neighbors see relatively few visitors even on a day when James Peak and St. Mary's Glacier are hosting throngs of climbers and skiers. Easy access, a scenic approach and fine skiing combine to make Bancroft a "must do" peak for ski and snowboard mountaineers. The two alpine basins on the east side of Bancroft contain six beautiful lakes, the first of which, Loch Lomond, is a reservoir that is accessible in the summer by a 4WD road.

"Bancroft Bowl" on the east side of the mountain has two ski descent routes. To reach the bowl and the final route to the summit, drive west from the Alice subdivision on Stewart Road until the road becomes impassable due to snow or rocks. The first one-third mile of Stewart Road is 2WD but turns into 4WD near a huge tailings pile at 10,400'. Park and then ski or hike toward Loch Lomond along the remainder of this scenic road. Take a few moments along the way to study the peaks and valleys that comprise the drainages to the south.

About a quarter mile before reaching the Loch Lomond dam, veer left (west) and head up into Bancroft Bowl. (Note that the craggy ridge west of Loch Lomond leads to a false summit northeast of Bancroft. The true summit sits to the left and appears lower and less distinct.) Pass about 100 yards north of the rocky nubbin 11,942'. From here two routes to the summit are possible. You can head on snow directly west up the bowl and then slant left to reach the southeast ridge at elevation 12,600.' A more scenic and breezier route involves climbing onto the snow-free southeast ridge soon after passing the rocky nubbin. Once on the southeast ridge follow it to the summit.

Bancroft Bowl Direct - Advanced

This steeper descent drops over 1000 vertical feet to the west end of Lake Caroline. It is free of cornices and isn't as steep as it looks. To reach the bowl from the summit, ski about 150 yards northeast down the summit ridge to the top of the bowl. Ski down to the west end of Lake Caroline, ski around the south shore, and then continue downhill another 600 vertical feet to the west shore of Loch Lomond. From Loch Lomond ski past the dam about one-third mile and pick up the approach route and reverse it back to your car. If time permits you can spend the afternoon touring the lovely lakes above Loch Lomond before returning.

Southside - Intermediate

This descent has 200 fewer vertical feet than the Direct route but is less intimidating (around 25 degrees). From the summit retrace your steps (or ski) down the southeast ridge to 12,800'. From here you can drop into the bowl and ski toward Lake Caroline. Continue as for the Direct route above.

Mount Bancroft from the northeast. "Bancroft Bowl" is the snow slope that lies to the left of the summit.

PARRY PEAK (13,391')

Starting Elevation .. 10,225'
Elevation Gain .... 3,166'
Distance .... 7.0 miles
U.S.G.S. Map .... Empire
Access Point .... Fall River Reservoir Road
Best Months .... May/June
Map .... Page 139
Rating .... Advanced

Many people drive to Fall River Reservoir and nearby Chinns Lake, to fish and view the surrounding peaks. Fewer people continue above the lakes to climb and ski. Of the peaks that stretch south from James Peak to Berthoud Pass, Parry is the tallest. Certainly when viewed from the valley below, the snow covered southeast face of Parry Peak appears to be a daunting line to ski. In truth advanced skiers will find both the climb and the descent of Parry Peak extremely satisfying.

Drive as far as possible along the dirt road that leads toward Fall River Reservoir from the paved Fall River Road. The road is in relatively good condition as far as the millsite at elevation 10,225' just past the bridge across Fall River. Beyond this point snowbanks and meltwater may be present in late May or early June. There is little value in pushing your luck further up valley, so park, heave your gear on your back and head along the road to the reservoir which lies 1.5 miles further.

At the reservoir, stand on the south end of the dam and check your map. It might appear that to reach the upper valley you should skirt the reservoir and climb the steep slope at its west end. Actually a better route is to walk north along the dam, head north uphill through a slot in the trees to around 11,000', then veer northwest and eventually west along open slopes that will deposit you on the north side of the upper basin.

The south face of Parry Peak viewed from the summit of Mount Eva.
Parry's southeast-facing descent route is located to the right of the summit.

MOUNT EVA (13,130')

Starting Elevation .. **10,225'**
Elevation Gain .... **2,905'**
Distance .... **6.5 miles**
U.S.G.S. Map .... **Empire**
Access Point .... **Fall River Reservoir Road**
Best Months .... **May/June**
Map .... **Page 139**
Rating .... **Intermediate or Advanced**

Mount Eva is the snowy temptress that comes in and out of view as one heads up the Fall River drainage. Actually it is Eva's jutting east ridge that is erroneously identified as Eva; for Eva's true summit is hidden further west. Early in the season with her flanks streaked by steep strips of snow (go ahead – say it fast), we have pondered the potential for sensational ski descents. But with time these apparent descents proved ephemeral as these lines melted quickly and were prone to slide on their slabby rock beds. So how does one climb and ski Eva? There are two ways. On the south face below and slightly east of the summit there are 1,200 vertical feet of snow that comprise an advanced ski route. One can also climb Eva and ski down the intermediate bowl ("Eva Bowl") that faces east between Eva and Mount Witter.

For either of these routes you must reach the bowl below Eva's south face. This is not difficult, and there are two choices. The first is to park at the millsite on the Fall River Reservoir Road as described for Parry Peak. Head 0.6 mile along the road to where the 4WD road to Chinns Lake forks to the left. Veer left onto this road and walk or ski one mile to the dam at Chinn's Lake. Continue west along the north shores of both Chinns and Sherwin Lakes. From the west end of Sherwin Lake climb steeply west up the open drainage to where it flattens; then turn northwest and ski into the Eva-Witter Bowl.

Or…drive as far as possible up the rocky Fall River Road (4WD) that leads to Fall River Reservoir. Park, continue up the road to the dam, turn left (south) up the steep wooded slope and climb 200 vertical feet to Chinns Lake. Continue as for option one above.

From the flat bottom of the bowl, there are two routes to the summit of Eva. You can head west-northwest to the Continental Divide along the path of least resistance and then follow the southwest ridge to the summit. Or climb north-northwest up the snow slopes that lead to the 12,800' saddle slightly east of the summit which can then be reached via a short step.

The summit has excellent closeup views of Parry Peak to the north and Mount Witter to the south. The top of Berthoud Pass is also visible as are the Winter Park Ski area and the entire Fraser Valley.

Southeast Face - Advanced

This route descends 1,200 vertical feet and retraces the second ascent route described above. Another way to descend from the summit begins at the U-notch in front of the steel tower along the southwest ridge. The U-notch provides a break in the cornice that rims the summit ridge and clearly is safer than wrestling with the cornice.

Another way to reach the summit and the southeast face is to climb the northfacing snowfield that lies slightly east of the summit. This snowfield can be reached by following directions to Parry Peak. From the approach to the base of Parry's southeast face (described earlier) locate Eva's northfacing snow slope and climb it to the summit ridge.

Eva Bowl - Intermediate

The easiest way down on skis is to retrace the first ascent route described above. This bowl becomes patchy around the end of May and it may be necessary to travel on foot for short stretches. But, if your appetite for turns is unsatisfied in the bowl, note that there is more intermediate skiing on the slopes west of Sherwin Lake.

Because the approach for Eva is relatively short, you might consider following a descent of Eva with an ascent and descent of Mount Witter. With all the options presented above, be sure to bring along a coin to flip.

Mount Eva from the east. The true summit is hidden from view.

WITTER PEAK (12,884')

Starting Elevation .. 10,225'
Elevation Gain .... 2,659'
Distance .... 6.7 miles
U.S.G.S. Map .... Empire
Access Point .... Fall River Reservoir Road
Best Months .... May/June
Map .... Page 139
Rating .... Advanced

An ascent and descent of Witter Peak can be combined with a trip to Eva or it can be done alone. Because of its lower elevation the ascent is short and the ski descent, while just under 1,000 feet, is steep enough to be challenging and satisfying. The bowl on Witter's north side can be reached by following the description provided earlier for Mount Eva.

As seen from the bowl, there may be more than one snowslope present on Witter's north flank. Check the map for help in identifying the correct snowslope. The correct slope reaches the west ridge at a point one-quarter mile west of the summit. This slope may be climbed more directly or it may be easier to climb the steep rock-strewn tundra slopes to the left of the snow.

Once the west ridge has been gained, the summit lies a scenic one-quarter mile further east. There is a tremendous view into the complex upper Mill Creek drainage. Looking eastward see if you can spot I-70 where it tops out over Mount Vernon Canyon. And finally, enjoy the descent back to Sherwin Lake.

Mount Witter and Mount Eva from the north. This photograph was taken along Stewart Road on the way to Loch Lomond.

REGION 6

Cascade Creek

This region (actually a single, long valley) is the only region of the Indian Peaks west of the Continental Divide that we have chosen to describe. We have explored the west side of the Indian Peaks and haven't found enough satisfactory routes that would justify the long approaches that would be required. This region is a notable exception. In early to mid-June you can backpack on a snowfree trail as far as Mirror and Cascade Lakes and camp just below the lakes. From the beginning of the trail at Monarch Lake to its end near Mirror Lake, the scenery is absolutely lovely. The scenic highlight is the symmetric, pointed pinnacle known as Lone Eagle which is a destination for climbers later in the summer. But for now, in early June, this area is yours. There is excellent skiing above Cascade Lake. Further along the valley Fair Glacier provides one of the most outstanding ski descents in the Indian Peaks.

Cascade Falls situated along the Cascade Creek Trail

CRATER LAKE &
LONE EAGLE CIRQUE (10,320')

Starting Elevation .. 8,340'
Elevation Gain .... 1,980'
Distance.................. 8 miles
U.S.G.S. Map .... Monarch Lake
Access Point........... Monarch Lake
Best Months .... June or July
Map .... Page 140
Rating...................... Advanced

An overnight trip to the upper reaches of Cascade Creek on the west side of the Continental Divide is a complete ski mountaineering experience. Steep-sided valleys, dense timber, thundering waterfalls, emerging wildflowers, and sunlit meadows are preludes to the area's centerpiece, Lone Eagle Peak. This polished pinnacle and the two great cirques that flank it constitute the most breathtaking scenery in the Indian Peaks. For the ski mountaineer who is willing to pack in a couple nights' provisions plus ski gear, the rewards are solitude, great scenery, and two fine ski descents. Plan to devote a full and satisfying day just to hiking in.

From the Monarch Lake parking area, follow the Cascade Trail along the north shore of the lake for a mile and enter the forest. Pass junctions with the Southside and Buchanan Trails as you ascend the well crafted trail up into the meadows at the foot of Cascade Falls. Passing the tremendous waterfall, the trail steepens with tantalizing glimpses of the high country that lies ahead. Further along, crossing the wide, gushing outlet of Pawnee Lake may be problematic. At the beginning of June, snowline will be reached just above 10,000 feet. Consider donning skis and skins or else brace yourself for a mile of agonizing postholing. Soon a junction with the Crater Lake trail and the Cascade Trail branching left toward Pawnee Pass is reached. Continue straight ahead on the Crater Lake trail. Map in hand, watch for a meadow (10,200') just north of and across from the Mirror Lake outlet. There is a log bridge in this area, but it could be snow covered. With luck you may find a dry campsite nearby. Dry campsites are even more sparse around Crater Lake. From this meadow it is an easy and obvious hop to Mirror and Crater Lakes.

"Lone Rabbit" (12,000') - Advanced

Between Mount Achonee and Lone Eagle there is a large basin with Crater Lake at its foot. Tucked into the southeast corner of this basin is tiny Peck Glacier, a mere shred of the alpine glacier that once filled the basin, and, in fact, the whole of upper Cascade Creek.

Stand on the northeast shore of Crater Lake and locate Peck Glacier just right of Lone Eagle. The upper reach of the glacier is a cornice-capped hourglass couloir that extends to the ridgetop. The run we've named "Lone Rabbit" starts along the horizontal line of snow to the left of this couloir and runs continuously for 1,600 vertical feet to the southeast shore of Crater Lake. The very top of the run is very steep but very short and quickly moderates to a more comfortable grade (30-35 degrees).

Memorial Day. "Lone Rabbit" rises above Cascade Lake. Lone Eagle is partially visible to the left. Peck Glacier is nestled high up in the notch a bit right of center.

To reach Peck Glacier and "Lone Rabbit," walk to the outlet of Crater Lake and gingerly cross the outlet on a logjam. Head south out of the trees and angle up toward the base of Lone Eagle on a line that intersects "Lone Rabbit" at 10,600'. Here the terrain flattens for 100 yards before ascending steeply up a second long snow pitch. (Keep an eye out for the Rabbit. He's watching the Eagle.) This second snow pitch tops out at the base of Peck Glacier. Continue as far up the glacier's headwall as your nerves and skills allow before taking the plunge. Stay clear of the runout zone beneath the aforementioned couloir.

Fair Glacier (12,400') - Expert

To travel into the stark bastion of Fair Glacier is an otherworldly experience. Towering at the head of a narrow cirque east of Lone Eagle, Fair Glacier defies descent. But for ski mountaineers with the drive to reach its base and the energy to climb it, *Fair* Glacier belies its name – in reality it's *excellent*. As is so often the case when viewing snowslopes head on, it's not as steep as it looks. The lower half is 30-35 degrees up to 12,200' and 40-45 degrees to the top. The total descent from the top of the glacier to Triangle Lake is 1,400 vertical feet.

To reach Fair Glacier from a 10,200' camp below Mirror Lake, cross Cascade Creek on a log bridge and head upstream to the Mirror Lake outlet stream. Cross the outlet stream wherever feasible, then head back upstream along Cascade Creek and cross it as soon as possible. (This circuitous route avoids the maze of house-sized boulders on the east bank of Cascade Creek.) Once back on the east side of Cascade Creek, climb a few steps to higher ground then walk or ski up the beautiful park-like valley. Note the puppet-like rock formations on the ridgetop to the left. At the end of this flat valley, turn right and clamber up the big talus that entombs the outlet of Triangle Lake. Catch your breath at the lake (10,980').

From here head around the west end of the lake and the rest of the route is a steep snow climb and obvious. From the top of the glacier, one can drop skis and scramble west 200 yards to the unimposing summit of Mount George (12,876'). The sheer-sided 12,799' summit located two-thirds of a mile northwest is nick-named "Iroquois."

Early in June it is possible to ski back down to Triangle Lake. There are two precautions. First, the snow near the top of the glacier may not be sufficiently consolidated in early June to be skied safely or enjoyably. Second, a crevasse lurks below the snow at 12,200' but is likely to be solidly bridged in June. This crevasse opens up later in the summer when the snow overlying the glacier has melted away exposing the ice.

You'll be pleased to learn that the horizontal distance from the lake to the glacier's base appears foreshortened when viewed from the lake. Actually there's a terrific stretch of low angle cruising once you're off the glacier itself. Regardless of how much of the glacier you choose to ski, you won't regret your attempt. You can squeeze 300 more vertical feet of skiing out of your return trip by skirting the big talus below the lake. Instead of descending the talus, veer right (east) onto a boulder-strewn bench that leads north to a snow slope that faces directly downvalley. Crank out a few more turns before gliding back to camp.

Lone Eagle spire with Fair Glacier in the background. The snow-dusted mountain that looms to the left of Fair Glacier is Apache Peak. This is one of the most beautiful sights in Colorado. We camped here for three days on Memorial Day weekend and saw only one other person.

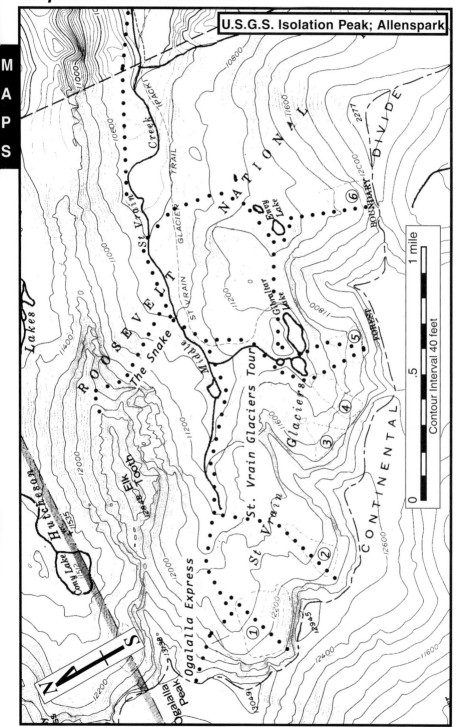

U.S.G.S. Isolation Peak; Allenspark

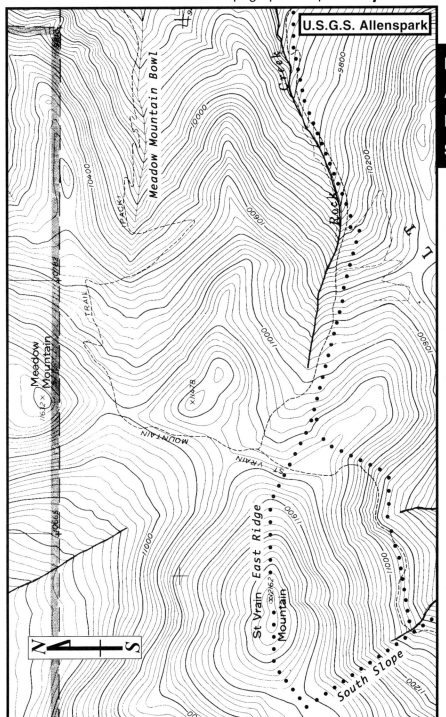

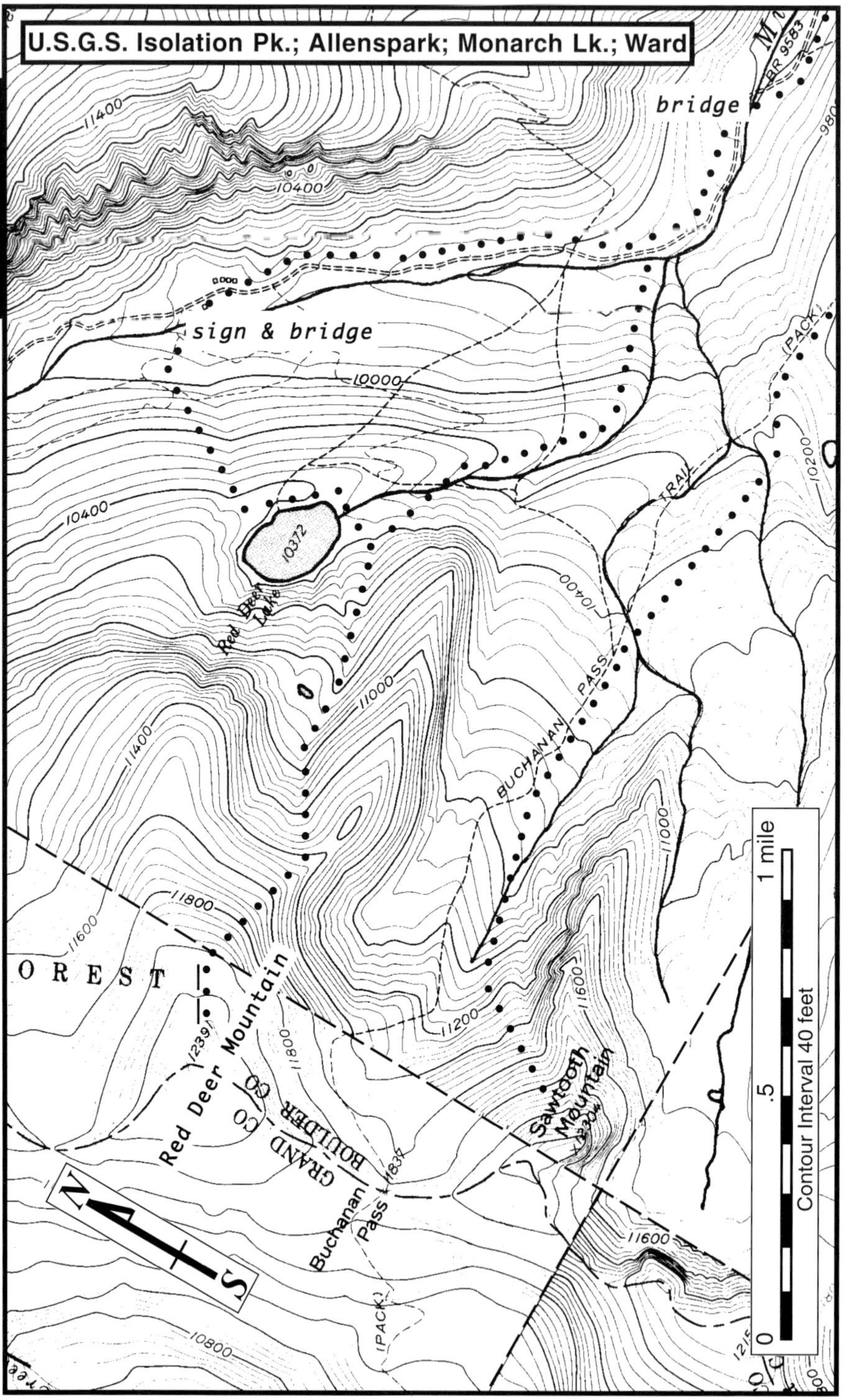
U.S.G.S. Isolation Pk.; Allenspark; Monarch Lk.; Ward
bridge
sign & bridge
BR 9583
11400
10400
10000
10372
Red Deer Lake
11000
10400
BUCHANAN PASS
TRAIL
(PACK)
10200
11400
11800
11600
OREST
Red Deer Mountain
12391
11800
GRAND CO
BOULDER CO
11837
Buchanan Pass
11200
Sawtooth Mountain
12304
11600
11000
11600
(PACK)
10800
N
S
1 mile
.5
0
Contour Interval 40 feet

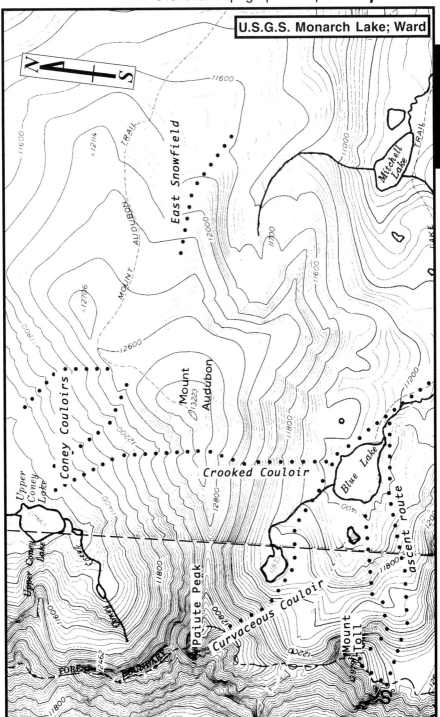

M A P S

Map...132 Indian Peak Descents

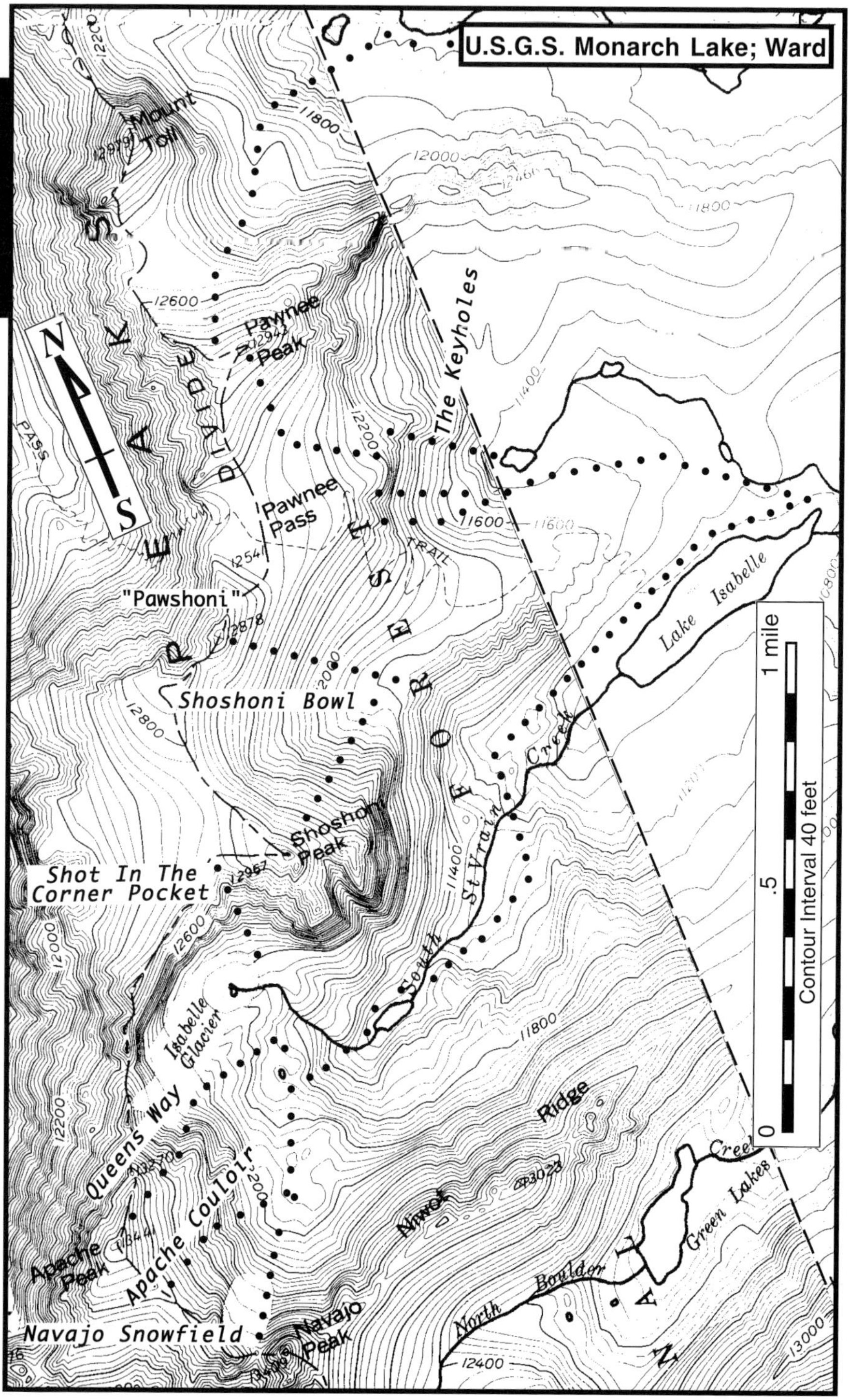

U.S.G.S. Monarch Lake; Ward

Mount Toll

Pawnee Peak

DIVIDE

The Keyholes

PASS

Pawnee Pass

TRAIL

"Pawshoni"

ISABELLE

Shoshoni Bowl

Lake Isabelle

Shoshoni Peak

Shot In The Corner Pocket

South St Vrain Creek

Isabelle Glacier

Queens Way

Ridge

Apache Peak

Apache Couloir

Niwot

Green Lakes

Navajo Snowfield

Navajo Peak

North Boulder Creek

1 mile

.5

Contour Interval 40 feet

0

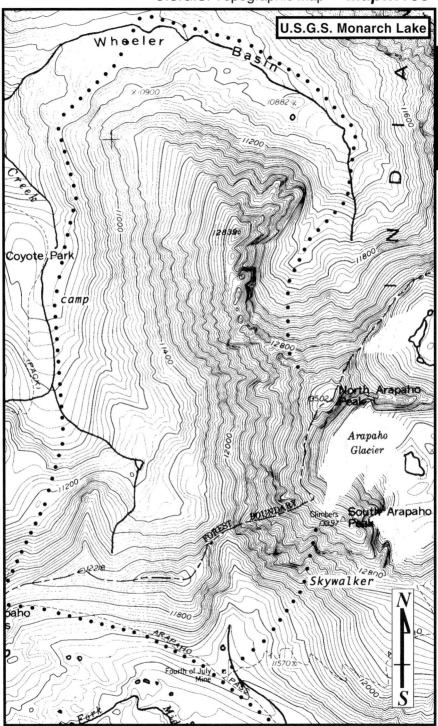

M
A
P
S

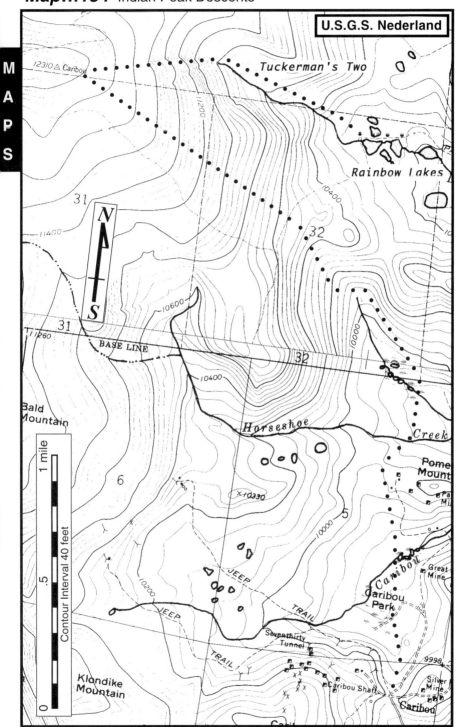

U.S.G.S. Nederland

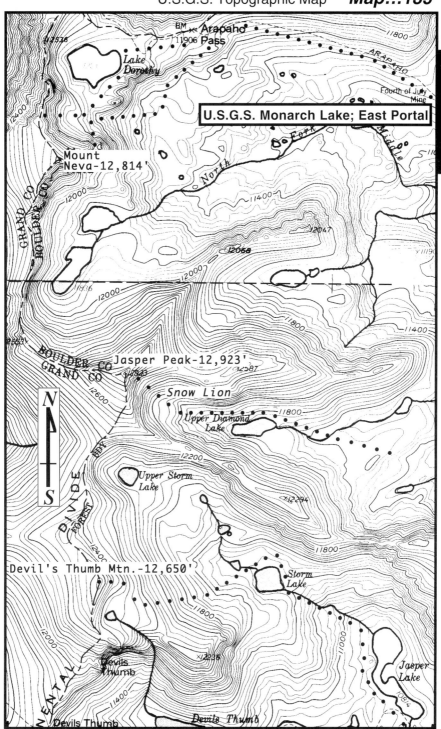

U.S.G.S. Monarch Lake; East Portal

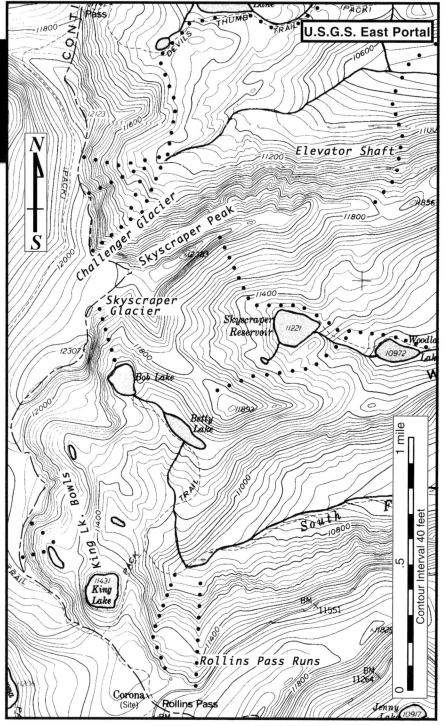

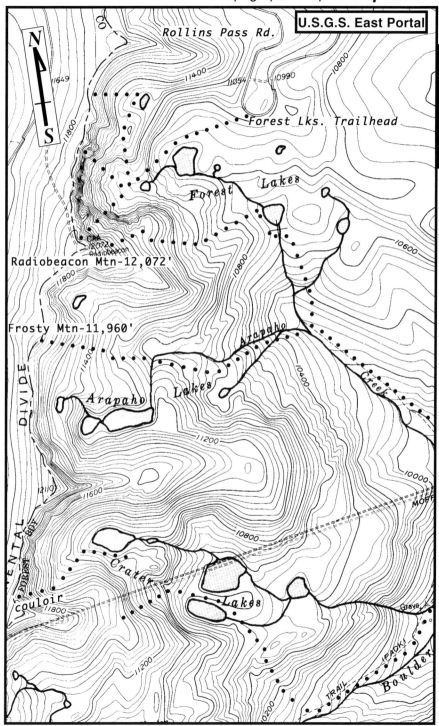

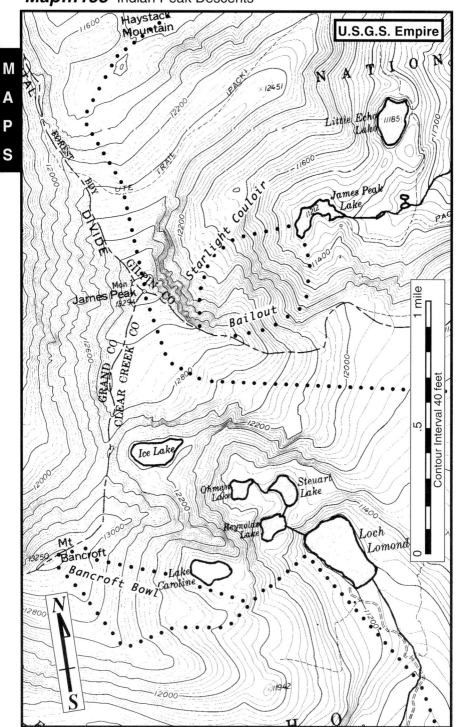

U.S.G.S. Empire

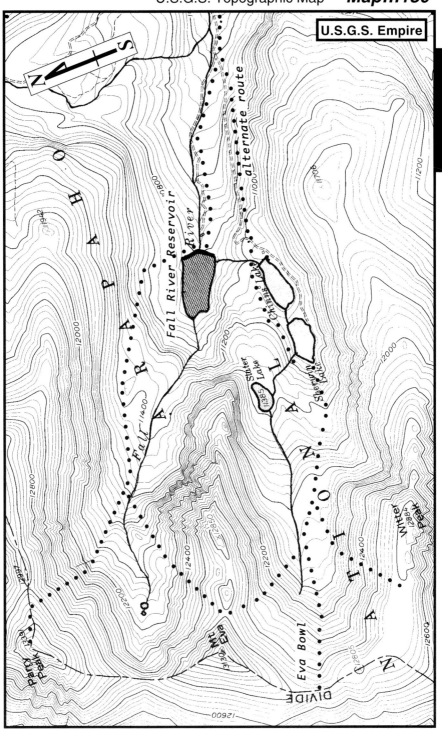

M
A
P
S

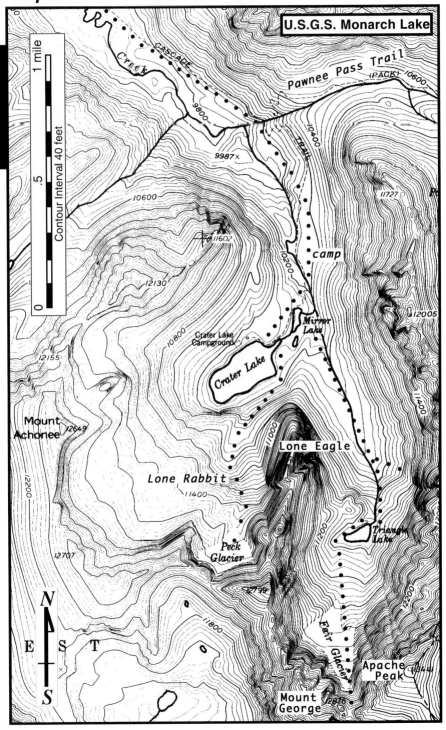

U.S.G.S. Monarch Lake

CASCADE

Creek

Pawnee Pass Trail (PACK) 10600

9800

10400

TRAIL

9987 ×

10600

11727

11602

10200

camp

12130

12005

10800

Mirror Lake

Crater Lake Campground

Crater Lake

12155

11400

Mount Achonee 12649

Lone Eagle

Lone Rabbit 11400

12200

Triangle Lake

Peck Glacier

11200

12200

12707

11000

12799

Fair Glacier

11800

Apache Peak

Mount George

1 mile

Contour Interval 40 feet

.5

0

N
E   S   T
S

Easternmost couloir on Mount Neva

The Peaks In Order of Elevation

North Arapaho Peak .... 13,502'

Apache Peak .... 13,441'

Navajo Peak .... 13,409'

South Arapaho Peak .... 13,397'

Parry Peak .... 13,391'

James Peak .... 13,294'

Mount Bancroft .... 13,250'

Mount Audubon .... 13,223'

Ogalalla Peak .... 13,138'

Mount Eva .... 13,130'

Paiute Peak .... 13,088'

Mount Toll .... 12,979'

Shoshoni Peak .... 12,967'

Pawnee Peak .... 12,943'

Jasper Peak .... 12,923'

Witter Peak .... 12,884'

"Pawshoni" .... 12,878'

Mount George .... 12,876'

Elk Tooth .... 12,848'

Mount Neva .... 12,814'

James Peak .... 12,800'

"Devil's Thumb Mountain" 12,650'

"Red Deer Mountain" .... 12,391'

"Skyscraper Peak" .... 12,383'

Caribou .... 12,310'

Sawtooth Mountain .... 12,304'

St. Vrain Mountain .... 12,162'

"Radiobeacon Mountain" ... 12,072'

"Frosty Mountain" .... 11,960'

Obtaining Topographic Maps

The maps that were reproduced in this book were taken from U.S.G.S. 7.5 minute (1:24,000) maps. The reproductions are not adequate for use in the backcountry. They are intended only as a guide to locating routes. Always carry a full-sized topographic map during your outings.

The following U.S.G.S. 7.5 minute quadrangles cover the Indian Peaks:

Allens Park	40105-B5-TF-024-00
Central City	39105-G5-TF-024-00
East Portal	39105-F8-TF-024-00
Empire	39105-G6-TF-024-00
Isolation Peak	40105-B6-TF-024-00
Monarch Lake	40105-A6-TF-024-00
Nederland	39105-H5-TF-024-00
Ward	40105-A5-TF-024-00

The Trails Illustrated *Indian Peaks – Gold Hill* map (Map #102) covers the Indian Peaks from Rocky Mountain National Park to Rollins Pass. This map is an excellent source of information.

U.S.G.S. maps and the Trails Illustrated map can be purchased at outdoor shops all along the Front Range, in Summit County, and in Winter Park and Fraser. Call ahead to check on availability since the more popular maps may be out of stock.

U.S.G.S. maps can also be ordered by mail from U.S.G.S., Information Services, Box 25286 Denver, CO 80225. For information about maps call 1-800-USA-MAPS. For help in ordering call 1-800-HELP-MAP.

Ski Equipment Dealers

Backcountry Access, 4949 Broadway, Boulder 303-417-1345
The Boulder Mountaineer, 1335 Broadway, Boulder 303-442-8355
Boulder Ski Deals, 2404 Pearl Street, Boulder 303-938-8799
Eastern Mountain Sports, 2550 Arapahoe Ave., Boulder 303-442-7566
Eastern Mountain Sports, 1616 Weston Street, Denver 303-446-8338
Grand West Outfitters, 801 Broadway, Denver 303-825-0300
The Mountain Shop, 632 S. Mason, Fort Collins 970-493-5720
Neptune Mountaineering, Table Mesa Center, Boulder 303-499-8866
The North Face, 2490 S. Colorado Blvd., Denver 303-758-6366
The North Face, 629 S. Broadway, Boulder 303-499-1731
R.E.I., 5375 S. Wadsworth Blvd., Lakewood 303-932-0600
R.E.I., 4100 E. Mexico Ave. (Bldg. C), Denver 303-756-3100
R.E.I., 8991B Harlan Street, Westminster 303-429-1800

Permit Issuing Locations

Boulder Ranger District
USDA Forest Service
2995 Baseline Road, Room 110
Boulder, CO 80303
303-444-6600
Mon-Fri 8-5

Sulphur Ranger District
USDA Forest Service
62429 U.S. Highway 40
P.O. Box 10
Granby, CO 80446
303-887-3331
Summer: Mon-Fri 8-5

Coast To Coast Hardware
Village Shopping Center
Nederland, CO 80466
303-258-3132
Mon-Sat 8-8
Sun 9-5

Estes Park Office
USDA Forest Service
161 Second Street
Estes Park, CO 80517
Summer: Sun-Sat 8-5

Monarch Lake Wilderness Station
(located by the outlet of Monarch Lake)
Sun-Sat 8-5
Day-of-trip permits only

Important Phone Numbers

In An Emergency

In case of an emergency, call the County Sheriff closest to the accident scene.

Boulder County Sheriff 303-441-4444
Clear Creek County Sheriff 303-569-3251
Gilpin County Sheriff 303-582-5511
Grand County Sheriff 970-725-3344

Road Condition Report

303-639-1111 (within two hours of Denver)
303-639-1234 (statewide)

National Forest Road Information

Boulder Ranger District 303-444-6600
Clear Creek Ranger District 303-567-2901
Sulphur Ranger District 303-887-3331

Books and Videos

Mountaineering is among the richest of human endeavors. Aside from developing and using the skills needed to reach your objective and return safely, a mountaineer has an enormous opportunity to learn about and appreciate the mountain environment.

How did the mountains develop, and why are they shaped a certain way? Why does the snow settle where it does? How is the vegetation patterned? Who are the birds and mammals that call out and scurry by as we pass? What is a ladybug doing in the middle of an immense snowfield? Observe, question, think, learn, appreciate. Get to know the geology and natural history of these mountains.

To assist you in getting to know the Indian Peaks more intimately, the list that follows contains a broader range of references than one finds in a typical "guidebook."

Geology, Natural History, and Human History

Arps, Louisa W., and Elinor Kingery. *High Country Names*. Boulder: Johnson Books, 1994...For trivia lovers and local history buffs.

Benedict, Audrey D. *A Sierra Club Naturalist's Guide: The Southern Rockies*. San Francisco: Sierra Club Books, 1991...Beautifully written, comprehensive guide to geology, meteorology, and natural history.

Chronic, Halka. *Roadside Geology of Colorado*. Missoula: Mountain Press, 1980...A great way to get the "big picture." Keep it in your car.

Craighead, John J., Frank C. Craighead, Jr., and Ray Davis. *A Field Guide To Rocky Mountain Wildflowers*. (Peterson Field Guide Series) Boston: Houghton Mifflin Co. 1974...Color photographs along with written descriptions and line drawings. Ninety percent of the flowers that you'll see can be quickly identified.

Mutel, Cornelia and John C. Emerick. *From Grassland To Glacier: The Natural History of Colorado*. Boulder: Johnson Books, 1992...A classic that focuses on the diversity of Colorado's major ecosystem units.

Ski Mountaineering, Ski Touring, and Climbing In Colorado

Barton, Harlan N. *Peak To Peak, Colorado Front Range Ski Trails.* Boulder: Front Range Publishing, 1995...A fact filled ski touring guide that includes an excellent map.

Dawson, Louis W. *Colorado High Routes.* Seattle: The Mountaineers, 1986...Mostly advanced, strenuous routes in central Colorado.

Dawson, Louis W. *Guide To Colorado's Fourteeners: Vols. 1&2.* Monument, CO: Blue Clover Press, 1994/6...Meticulously documented and extremely well researched. Contains information on technical routes, snow climbs and ski descents. Lou has climbed and skied every Fourteener.

Litz, Brian and Kurt Lankford. *Skiing Colorado's Backcountry: Northern Mountains - Trails and Tours.* Golden: Fulcrum, 1989...The best coverage of routes from novice to expert over a broad region.

Roach, Gerry. *Colorado's Indian Peaks Wilderness Area: Classic Hikes and Climbs.* Golden: Fulcrum, 1989...A terrific resource packed into a tiny book.

Ski Mountaineering Beyond Colorado

Cliff, Peter. *Ski Mountaineering.* Seattle: Pacific Search Press, 1987...This well illustrated textbook on ski mountaineering covers the globe.

Moynier, John. *Backcountry Skiing in the High Sierra.* Evergreen: Chockstone Press, 1992...Contains a final section on mouth-watering peak descents.

Skiing Techniques and General Mountaineering

Graydon, Don (Editor). *Mountaineering: The Freedom of the Hills.* Seattle: The Mountaineers: 1992...The best single source for information and techniques related to mountain travel. A well respected classic.

Parker, Paul. *Free-Heel Skiing.* Seattle, The Mountaineers. 1995...The next best thing to a private lesson with Paul.

Tejada-Flores, Lito. *Breakthrough On Skis*. New York: Vintage Books. 1994...An indispensable book for alpine skiers who want to climb out of the intermediate rut.

Periodicals

BackCountry, Four issues per year. Subscribe to Backcountry Publishing, Inc. 7065 Dover Way, Arvada, CO 80004. $9.95 per year.

Couloir, Four issues per year. Subscribe to Couloir Publications, P.O. Box 2048, Simi Valley, CA 93062. $12.00 per year

Both of these periodicals are practical as well as inspirational. In a word, subscribe.

Videotapes

There are very few videos that focus on ski mountaineering and/or free-heel skiing. The three best works have been produced by the North American Telemark Organization (NATO) which is based in Waitsfield, Vermont. Dick Hall (NATO's founder) and Mark Fuller (a ski instructor and cinematographer) have created three videos that combine technical instruction, breathtaking scenery, appropriate music, and humorous moments. Buy or rent any or all of them.

The Telemark Movie. Silver Springs: Telemark Films, 1987 (70 mins.)

Revenge of the Telemarkers. Waitsfield: Telemark Movies Inc. 1989 (75 mins.)

The Telemark Workshop. Waitsfield: Telemark Movies Inc. 1992 (30 mins.)

The Backcountry Skiers Alliance

The BSA was formed in an effort to preserve the quality of the non-motorized backcountry experience and to maintain the integrity of the Colorado backcountry by helping to resolve conflicts between motorized and non-motorized users. BSA is a non-profit, membership organization. For more information on BSA or to join, write to:

Backcountry Skiers Alliance
P.O. Box 134
Boulder, CO 80306

A Parting Shot...

We had just spent three perfect days by ourselves camping and skiing in Lone Eagle Cirque. The afternoon of the last day we took down our camp at snowline, heaved our packs on our backs and began the ten mile trudge back to our car at the far end of Monarch Lake.

Monarch Lake and Buchanan Creek at dusk

It's at times like these that we wonder if it's at all possible to describe an experience like this to another person – even a person who has enjoyed similar experiences. How do you verbalize or photograph the scent of a warm forest, or the sound of skis "shooshing" over cold, wet velvet? What about a scene, such as a thundering waterfall, so beautiful that it strains the eyes to look away? Do you know the feel of hot cocoa warming icy fingers at 5:00 am? Can you describe it?

This book – any guidebook, for that matter – provides only a crude sketch of what it's like to spend a day in the mountains. This has been our greatest challenge in writing this book.

About The Authors...

On the summit of Apache Peak

Ron Haddad is a Boulder Valley resident who works as a Science teacher. His classroom offers a view of the Indian Peaks. He is a year-round skier who has enjoyed ski mountaineering experiences during the past fifteen years in Colorado, Utah, Montana, California, New York and New Hampshire. He has a passion for poring over maps in search of potential ski descents and then testing his hunches. Ron has skied all of the routes in this book as well as many other routes in Colorado.

Eileen Faughey is a Boulder nutrition consultant whose lifelong love for wilderness travel has taken her to the mountains in twelve states and seven countries. She is an avid downhill and backcountry skier who has logged hundreds of miles of skiing in Colorado's wild backcountry.

Eileen and Ron have shared with each other the joys of wilderness travel for the past eighteen years. This book is their attempt to share with its readers a "slice" of that joy.

Peter Bridge

Slope Steepness Table

For determining slope angles using 1:24,000 (7.5 minute) U.S.G.S. topographic maps. Keep in mind that the steepness values in the table are averages. For example, it is quite possible that a slope that is shown to have an average steepness of 35° from the table could have a 50° section. The small millimeter ruler below the table may not be accurate because of imperfections in the printing process. Purchase a small plastic ruler for best results. Clip out the table and keep it with your maps. It's a great way to settle any "How steep do you think it is?" arguments.

Directions:

1. Measure the distance (in mm.) on your map between two or more 200 feet interval lines (the darker brown lines).

2. In the table, go down to the number of mm. measured and across to the column that corresponds to the interval in vertical feet.

3. The number in the box is the average steepness in degrees.

Example: (See *Map...137*) Locate the descent route on the southeast face of Skyscraper Peak. The distance between the 12,000' and 11,600' interval lines is 10 mm. From the table, the average steepness along this section is 27°.

mm	Vertical Feet Measured		
	200	400	600
2.0	52	68	75
2.5	45	64	72
3.0	40	59	68
3.5	36	55	65
4.0	32	52	62
4.5	29	48	59
5.0	27	45	57
5.5	25	42	54
6.0	23	40	52
6.5	21	38	49
7.0	20	36	47
7.5	19	34	45
8.0	17	32	43
8.5	17	31	42
9.0	16	29	40
9.5	15	28	39
10.0	14	27	37
10.5	13	26	36
11.0	13	25	34
11.5	12	24	33
12.0	12	23	32
12.5	11	22	31
13.0	11	21	30
13.5	11	20	29
14.0	10	20	28

◄ millimeter rule